Hand *to* Mouth

ALSO BY PAUL AUSTER

Novels
The New York Trilogy (City of Glass • Ghosts •
The Locked Room) • In the Country of Last Things •
Moon Palace • The Music of Chance • Leviathan •
Mr. Vertigo • Timbuktu • The Book of Illusions

Nonfiction
White Spaces • The Invention of Solitude • The Art of
Hunger • Why Write? • The Story of Mr. Typewriter (with
Sam Messer) • The Red Notebook

Screenplays
Smoke & Blue in the Face • Lulu on the Bridge

Poetry
Unearth • Wall Writing • Fragments from Cold • Facing
the Music • Disappearances: Selected Poems

Editor
The Random House Book of Twentieth-Century French
Poetry • I Thought My Father Was God: And Other True
Tales from NPR's National Story Project

Hand *to* Mouth

A Chronicle of Early Failure

Paul Auster

<u>Picador</u>
Henry Holt and Company
New York

www.picadorusa.com

Picador® is a U.S. registered trademark and is used by Henry Holt and Company under license from Pan Books Limited.

For information on Picador Reading Group Guides, as well as ordering, please contact the Trade Marketing department at St. Martin's Press.
Phone: 1-800-221-7945 extension 488
Fax: 212-677-7456
E-mail: trademarketing@stmartins.com

Library of Congress Cataloging-in-Publication Data

Auster, Paul, 1947–
    Hand to mouth : a chronicle of early failure / Paul Auster.
    —1st Picador pbk. ed.
        p.   cm.
    ISBN 0-312-42232-6
    1. Auster, Paul, 1947—Homes and haunts—New York (State)—New York. 2. Authors, American—Homes and haunts—New York (State)—New York. 3. Auster, Paul, 1947—Homes and haunts—France—Paris. 4. Authors, American—Homes and haunts—France—Paris.
    5. Americans—France—Paris—History 20th century.
    6. Authors, American—20th century—Biography.
    7. Authorship—Economic aspects.   I. Title.

PS3551.U77Z4616 2993
813'.54—dc21   2003040573

Book design by Nick Wunder

First published in the United States by Henry Holt and Company

D 10 9 8 7 6 5

Hand *to* Mouth

IN MY LATE twenties and early thirties, I went through a period of several years when everything I touched turned to failure. My marriage ended in divorce, my work as a writer foundered, and I was overwhelmed by money problems. I'm not just talking about an occasional shortfall or some periodic belt tightenings—but a constant, grinding, almost suffocating lack of money that poisoned my soul and kept me in a state of never-ending panic.

There was no one to blame but myself. My relationship to money had always been flawed, enigmatic, full of contradictory impulses, and now I was paying the price for refusing to take a clear-cut stand on the matter. All along, my only ambition had been to write.

I had known that as early as sixteen or seventeen years old, and I had never deluded myself into thinking I could make a living at it. Becoming a writer is not a "career decision" like becoming a doctor or a policeman. You don't choose it so much as get chosen, and once you accept the fact that you're not fit for anything else, you have to be prepared to walk a long, hard road for the rest of your days. Unless you turn out to be a favorite of the gods (and woe to the man who banks on that), your work will never bring in enough to support you, and if you mean to have a roof over your head and not starve to death, you must resign yourself to doing other work to pay the bills. I understood all that, I was prepared for it, I had no complaints. In that respect, I was immensely lucky. I didn't particularly want anything in the way of material goods, and the prospect of being poor didn't frighten me. All I wanted was a chance to do the work I felt I had it in me to do.

Most writers lead double lives. They earn good money at legitimate professions and carve out time for their writing as best they can: early in the morning, late at night, weekends, vacations. William Carlos Williams and Louis-Ferdinand Céline were doctors. Wallace Stevens worked for an insurance company. T. S. Eliot was a banker, then a publisher. Among my own acquaintances, the French poet Jacques Dupin is co-director of an art gallery in Paris. William Bronk, the American poet, managed his family's coal and lumber business in upstate New York for over forty years. Don DeLillo, Peter Carey, Salman Rushdie, and Elmore Leonard all worked for long stretches in advertising. Other writers teach. That is probably the most common solution today, and with every major university and Podunk college offering so-called creative writing courses, novelists and poets are continually scratching and scrambling to land themselves a spot. Who can blame them? The salaries might not be big, but the work is steady and the hours are good.

My problem was that I had no interest in leading a double life. It's not that I wasn't willing to work, but the idea of punching a clock at some nine-to-five job left me cold, utterly devoid of enthusiasm. I was in my early twenties, and I felt too young to settle down, too full of other plans to waste my time earning more money than I either wanted or needed. As far as finances went, I just wanted to get by. Life was cheap in those days, and with no responsibility for anyone but myself, I figured I could scrape along on an annual income of roughly three thousand dollars.

I tried graduate school for a year, but that was only because Columbia offered me a tuition-free fellowship with a two-thousand-dollar stipend—which meant that I was actually paid to study. Even under

those ideal conditions, I quickly understood that I
wanted no part of it. I had had enough of school, and
the prospect of spending another five or six years as
a student struck me as a fate worse than death. I
didn't want to talk about books anymore. I wanted to
write them. Just on principle, it felt wrong to me for
a writer to hide out in a university, to surround himself
with too many like-minded people, to get too comfortable. The risk was complacency, and once that
happens to a writer, he's as good as lost.

I'm not going to defend the choices I made. If they
weren't practical, the truth was that I didn't want to
be practical. What I wanted were new experiences. I
wanted to go out into the world and test myself, to
move from this to that, to explore as much as I could.
As long as I kept my eyes open, I figured that whatever happened to me would be useful, would teach
me things I had never known before. If this sounds
like a rather old-fashioned approach, perhaps it was.
Young writer bids farewell to family and friends and
sets out for points unknown to discover what he's made
of. For better or worse, I doubt that any other approach
would have suited me. I had energy, a head crammed
full of ideas, and itchy feet. Given how big the world
was, the last thing I wanted was to play it safe.

It's not difficult for me to describe these things and to remember how I felt about them. The trouble begins only when I question why I did them and why I felt what I felt. All the other young poets and writers in my class were making sensible decisions about their futures. We weren't rich kids who could depend on handouts from our parents, and once we left college, we would be out on our own for good. We were all facing the same situation, we all knew the score, and yet they acted in one way and I acted in another. That's what I'm still at a loss to explain. Why did my friends act so prudently, and why was I so reckless?

I came from a middle-class family. My childhood was comfortable, and I never suffered from any of the wants and deprivations that plague most of the human beings who live on this earth. I never went hungry, I never was cold, I never felt in danger of losing any of the things I had. Security was a given, and yet for all the ease and good fortune in the household, money was a subject of continual conversation and worry. Both of my parents had lived through the Depression, and neither one had fully recovered from those hard times. Each had been marked by the experience of not having enough, and each bore the wound in a different way.

My father was tight; my mother was extravagant. She spent; he didn't. The memory of poverty had not loosened its hold on his spirit, and even though his circumstances had changed, he could never quite bring himself to believe it. She, on the other hand, took great pleasure in those altered circumstances. She enjoyed the rituals of consumerism, and like so many Americans before her and since, she cultivated shopping as a means of self-expression, at times raising it to the level of an art form. To enter a store was to engage in an alchemical process that imbued the cash register with magical, transformative properties. Inexpressible desires, intangible needs, and unarticulated longings all passed through the money box and came out as real things, palpable objects you could hold in your hand. My mother never tired of reenacting this miracle, and the bills that resulted became a bone of contention between her and my father. She felt that we could afford them; he didn't. Two styles, two worldviews, two moral philosophies were in eternal conflict with each other, and in the end it broke their marriage apart. Money was the fault line, and it became the single, overpowering source of dispute between them. The tragedy was that they were both good people—attentive, honest, hardworking—and aside from that one ferocious battleground, they seemed to get along rather well. For the life of me I could never understand how such a relatively unimportant issue could cause so much trouble between them. But money, of course, is never just money. It's always something else, and it's always something more, and it always has the last word.

As a small boy, I was caught in the middle of this ideological war. My mother would take me shopping for clothes, sweeping me up in the whirlwind of her enthusiasm and generosity, and again and again I would allow myself to be talked into wanting the things she offered me—always more than I was expecting, always more than I thought I needed. It was impossible to resist, impossible not to enjoy how the clerks doted on her and hopped to her commands, impossible not to be carried away by the power of her performance. My happiness was always mixed with a large dose of anxiety, however, since I knew exactly what my father was going to say when he got the bill. And the fact was that he always said it. The inevitable outburst would come, and almost inevitably the matter would be resolved with my father declaring that the next time I needed something, he was the one who would take me shopping. So the moment would roll around to buy me a new winter jacket, say, or a new pair of shoes, and one night after dinner my father and I would drive off to a discount store located on a highway somewhere in the New Jersey darkness. I remember the glare of fluorescent lights in those places, the cinder-block walls, the endless racks of cheap men's clothing. As the jingle on the radio put it: "Robert Hall this season / Will tell you the reason—/ Low overhead / Bum, bum, bum / Low overhead!" When all is said and done, that song is as much a part of my childhood as the Pledge of Allegiance or the Lord's Prayer.

The truth was that I enjoyed this bargain hunting with my father as much as I enjoyed the buying sprees orchestrated by my mother. My loyalties were equally divided between my two parents, and there was never any question of pitching my tent in one camp or the other. My mother's approach was more appealing, perhaps, at least in terms of the fun and excitement it generated, but there was something about my father's stubbornness that gripped me as well, a sense of hard-won experience and knowledge at the core of his beliefs, an integrity of purpose that made him someone who never backed down, not even at the risk of looking bad in the eyes of the world. I found that admirable, and much as I adored my beautiful, endlessly charming mother for dazzling the world as she did, I also adored my father for resisting that same world. It could be maddening to watch him in action—a man who never seemed to care what others thought of him—but it was also instructive, and in the long run I think I paid more attention to those lessons than I ever realized.

As a young boy I fell into the mold of your classic go-getter. At the first sign of snow, I would run out with my shovel and start ringing doorbells, asking people if they would hire me to clear their driveways and front walks. When the leaves fell in October, I would be out there with my rake, ringing those same doorbells and asking about the lawns. At other times, when there was nothing to remove from the ground, I would inquire about "odd jobs." Straightening up the garage, cleaning out the cellar, pruning the hedges—whatever needed to be done, I was the man to do it. In the summer, I sold lemonade for ten cents a glass on the sidewalk in front of my house. I gathered up empty bottles from the kitchen pantry, loaded them in my little red wagon, and lugged them to the store to turn in for cash. Two cents for the small ones; five cents for the big. I mostly used my earnings to buy baseball cards, sports magazines, and comic books, and whatever was left over I would diligently put in my piggy bank, which was built in the shape of a cash register. I was truly the child of my parents, and I never questioned the principles that animated their world. Money talked, and to the degree that you listened to it and followed its arguments, you would learn to speak the language of life.

Once, I remember, I was in possession of a fifty-cent piece. I can't recall how I came to have that

coin—which was just as rare then as it is now—but
whether it had been given to me or whether I had
earned it myself, I have a keen sense of how much it
meant to me and what a large sum it represented. For
fifty cents in those days you could buy ten packs of
baseball cards, five comic books, ten candy bars, fifty
jawbreakers—or, if you preferred, various combina-
tions of all of them. I put the half-dollar in my back
pocket and marched off to the store, feverishly cal-
culating how I was going to spend my little fortune.
Somewhere along the way, however, for reasons that
still confound me, the coin disappeared. I reached
into my back pocket to check on it—knowing it was
there, just wanting to make sure—and the money was
gone. Was there a hole in my pocket? Had I accidentally slid the coin out of my pants the last time I'd
touched it? I have no idea. I was six or seven years
old, and I still remember how wretched I felt. I had
tried to be so careful, and yet for all my precautions,
I had wound up losing the money. How could I have
allowed such a thing to happen? For want of any logical explanation, I decided that God had punished me.
I didn't know why, but I was certain that the All-
Powerful One had reached into my pocket and
plucked out the coin Himself.

Little by little, I started turning my back on my parents. It's not that I began to love them less, but the world they came from no longer struck me as such an inviting place to live. I was ten, eleven, twelve years old, and already I was becoming an internal émigré, an exile in my own house. Many of these changes can be attributed to adolescence, to the simple fact that I was growing up and beginning to think for myself— but not all of them. Other forces were at work on me at the same time, and each one had a hand in pushing me onto the road I later followed. It wasn't just the pain of having to witness my parents' crumbling marriage, and it wasn't just the frustration of being trapped in a small suburban town, and it wasn't just the American climate of the late 1950s—but put them all together, and suddenly you had a powerful case against materialism, an indictment of the orthodox view that money was a good to be valued above all others. My parents valued money, and where had it gotten them? They had struggled so hard for it, had invested so much belief in it, and yet for every problem it had solved, another one had taken its place. American capitalism had created one of the most prosperous moments in human history. It had produced untold numbers of cars, frozen vegetables, and miracle shampoos, and yet Eisenhower was President, and the entire country had been turned into a gigantic television commercial, an incessant harangue to buy more, make more, spend more, to dance around the dollar-tree until you dropped dead from the sheer frenzy of trying to keep up with everyone else.

It wasn't long before I discovered that I wasn't the only person who felt this way. At ten, I stumbled across an issue of *Mad* magazine in a candy store in Irvington, New Jersey, and I remember the intense, almost stupefying pleasure I felt at reading those pages. They taught me that I had kindred spirits in this world, that others had already unlocked the doors I was trying to open myself. Fire hoses were being turned on black people in the American South, the Russians had launched the first Sputnik, and I was starting to pay attention. No, you didn't have to swallow the dogma they were trying to sell you. You could resist them, poke fun at them, call their bluff. The wholesomeness and dreary rectitude of American life were no more than a sham, a halfhearted publicity stunt. The moment you began to study the facts, contradictions bubbled to the surface, rampant hypocrisies were exposed, a whole new way of looking at things suddenly became possible. We had been taught to believe in "liberty and justice for all," but the fact was that liberty and justice were often at odds with one another. The pursuit of money had nothing to do with fairness; its driving engine was the social principle of "every man for himself." As if to prove the essential inhumanity of the marketplace, nearly all of its metaphors had been taken from the animal kingdom: dog eat dog, bulls and bears, the rat race, survival of the fittest. Money divided the world into winners and losers, haves and have-nots. That was an excellent arrangement for the winners, but what about the people who lost? Based on the evidence available to me, I gathered that they were to be cast aside and forgotten. Too bad, of course, but those were the breaks. If you construct a world so primitive as to make Darwin your leading philosopher and Aesop your leading poet, what else can you expect? It's a jungle out there, isn't it? Just look at that Dreyfus lion strolling down the middle of Wall Street. Could the message be any clearer? Either eat or be eaten. That's the law of the jungle, my friend, and if you don't have the stomach for it, then get out while you still can.

I was out before I was ever in. By the time I entered my teens, I had already concluded that the world of business would have to get along without me. I was probably at my worst then, my most insufferable, my most confused. I burned with the ardor of a newfound idealism, and the stringencies of the perfection I sought for myself turned me into a pint-sized puritan-in-training. I was repulsed by the outward trappings of wealth, and every sign of ostentation my

parents brought into the house I treated with scorn.
Life was unfair. I had finally figured this out, and
because it was my own discovery, it hit me with all
the force of a revelation. As the months went by, I
found it increasingly difficult to reconcile my good
luck with the bad luck of so many others. What had
I done to deserve the comforts and advantages that
had been showered on me? My father could afford
them—that was all—and whether or not he and my
mother fought over money was a small point in com-
parison to the fact that they had money to fight over
in the first place. I squirmed every time I had to get
into the family car—so bright and new and expensive,
so clearly an invitation to the world to admire how
well off we were. All my sympathies were for the
downtrodden, the dispossessed, the underdogs of the
social order, and a car like that filled me with
shame—not just for myself, but for living in a world
that allowed such things to be in it.

My first jobs don't count. My parents were still sup-
porting me, and I was under no obligation to fend for
myself or contribute to the family budget. The pressure was therefore off, and without any pressure, nothing important can ever be at stake. I was glad to have
the money I earned, but I never had to use it on nuts-

and-bolts necessities, I never had to worry about putting food on the table or not falling behind with the rent. Those problems would come later. For now I was just a high school kid looking for a pair of wings to carry me away from where I was.

At sixteen, I spent two months working as a waiter at a summer camp in upstate New York. The next summer, I worked at my uncle Moe's appliance store in Westfield, New Jersey. The jobs were similar in that most of the tasks were physical and didn't require much thought. If carrying trays and scraping dishes was somewhat less interesting than installing air conditioners and unloading refrigerators from forty-foot trailer trucks, I wouldn't want to make too big a point of it. This isn't a question of apples and oranges— but of two kinds of apples, both the same shade of green. Dull as the work might have been, however, I found both jobs immensely satisfying. There were too many colorful characters around, too many surprises, too many new thoughts to absorb for me to resent the drudgery, and I never felt that I was wasting my time just to earn a paycheck. The money was an important part of it, but the work wasn't just about money. It was about learning who I was and how I fit into the world.

Even at the camp, where my coworkers were all sixteen- and seventeen-year-old high school boys, the kitchen help came from a starkly different universe. Down-and-outs, Bowery bums, men with dubious histories, they had been rounded up from the New York streets by the owner of the camp and talked into accepting their low-paying jobs—which included two months of fresh air and free room and board. Most of them didn't last long. One day they would just disappear, wandering back to the city without bothering to say good-bye. A day or two later, the missing man would be replaced by a similar lost soul, who rarely lasted very long himself. One of the dishwashers, I remember, was named Frank, a grim, surly guy with a serious drinking problem. Somehow or other, we managed to become friends, and in the evening after work was done we would sometimes sit on the steps behind the kitchen and talk. Frank turned out to be a highly intelligent, well-read man. He had worked as an insurance agent in Springfield, Massachusetts, and until the bottle got the better of him, he had lived the life of a productive, tax-paying citizen. I distinctly remember not daring to ask him what had happened, but one evening he told me anyway, turning what must have been a complicated story into a short, dry account of the events that had done him in. In the space of sixteen months, he said, every person who had ever meant anything to him died. He sounded philosophical about it, almost as if he were talking about someone else, and yet there was an undertow of bitterness in his voice. First his parents, he said, then his wife, and then his two children. Diseases, accidents, and burials, and by the time they were all gone, it was as if his insides had shattered. "I just gave up," he said. "I didn't care what happened to me anymore, so I became a bum."

The following year, in Westfield, I made the acquaintance of several more indelible figures. Carmen, for example, the voluminously padded, wisecracking bookkeeper, who to this day is still the only woman I've known with a beard (she actually had to shave), and Joe Mansfield, the assistant repairman with two hernias and a ravaged Chrysler that had wiped out the odometer three times and was now up to 360,000 miles. Joe was sending two daughters through college, and in addition to his day job at the appliance store, he worked eight hours every night as a foreman in a commercial bakery, reading comic books beside the huge vats of dough so as not to fall asleep. He was the single most exhausted man I have ever met—and also one of the most energetic. He kept himself going by smoking menthol cigarettes and downing twelve to sixteen bottles of orange soda a day, but not once did I ever see him put a morsel of food in his mouth. If he ate lunch, he said, it would make him too tired and he would collapse. The hernias had come a few

years earlier, when he and two other men were carrying a jumbo refrigerator up a narrow flight of stairs.
The other men had lost their grip, leaving Joe to bear
the entire weight of the thing himself, and it was exactly then, as he struggled not to be crushed by the
several hundred pounds he was holding, that his tes-
ticles had shot up out of his scrotum. First one ball,
he said, and then the other. Pop . . . pop. He wasn't
supposed to lift heavy objects anymore, but every time
there was an especially large appliance to deliver, he
would come along and help us—just to make sure we
didn't kill ourselves.

The *us* included a nineteen-year-old redhead
named Mike, a tense, wiry shrimp with a missing index finger and one of the fastest tongues I had yet
encountered. Mike and I were the air conditioner in-
stallation team, and we spent a lot of time together in
the store van, driving to and from jobs. I never tired
of listening to the onslaught of loopy, unexpected
metaphors and outrageous opinions that came pouring
out of him whenever he opened his mouth. If he found
one of the customers too snotty, for example, he
wouldn't say "that person's an asshole" (as most
would) or "that person's stuck-up" (as some would),
but "that person acts as if his shit doesn't smell."
Young Mike had a special gift, and on several occa-
sions that summer I was able to see how well it served

him. Again and again we would enter a house to install an air conditioner, and again and again, just as we were in the middle of the job (screwing in the screws, measuring strips of caulking to seal up the window), a girl would walk into the room. It never seemed to fail. She was always seventeen, always pretty, always bored, always "just hanging around the house." The instant she appeared, Mike would turn on the charm. It was as if he knew she was going to come in, as if he had already rehearsed his lines and was fully prepared. I, on the other hand, was always caught with my guard down, and as Mike launched into his song and dance (a combination of bullshit, razzle-dazzle, and raw nerve), I would dumbly plod on with the work. Mike would talk, and the girl would smile. Mike would talk a little more, and the girl would laugh. Within two minutes they were old friends, and by the time I'd put the finishing touches on the job, they were swapping phone numbers and arranging where to meet on Saturday night. It was preposterous; it was sublime; it made my jaw drop. If it had happened only once or twice, I would have dismissed it as a fluke, but this scene was played out repeatedly, no less than five or six times over the course of the summer. In the end, I grudgingly had to admit that Mike was more than just lucky. He was someone who created his own luck.

In September, I started my senior year of high school. It was the last year I spent at home, and it was also the last year of my parents' marriage. Their breakup had been so long in coming that when the news was announced to me at the end of Christmas vacation, I wasn't upset so much as relieved.

It had been a mismatch from the start. If they hung in together as long as they did, it was more for "the children's sake" than for their own. I don't presume to have any answers, but I suspect that a decisive moment occurred two or three years before the end, when my father took over the grocery-shopping duties for the household. That was the last great money battle my parents fought, and it stands in my mind as the symbolic last straw, the thing that finally knocked the stuffing out of both of them. It was true that my mother enjoyed filling her cart at the local Shop-Rite until it was almost too heavy to push; it was true that she took pleasure in providing the treats my sister and I asked her for; it was true that we ate well at home and that the pantry was abundantly stocked. But it was also true that we could afford these things and that the family finances were in no way threatened by the sums my mother forked over at the checkout counter. In my father's eyes, however, her spending was out of control. When he finally put his foot down, it landed in the wrong place, and he wound up doing what no man should ever do to his wife. In effect, he relieved her of her job. From then on, he was the one who took responsibility for bringing food into the house. Once, twice, even three times a week, he would stop off somewhere on the way home from work (as if he didn't have enough to do already) and load up the back of his station wagon with groceries. The choice cuts of meat my mother had brought home were replaced by chuck and shoulder. Name-brand products became generic products. After-school snacks vanished. I don't remember hearing my mother complain, but it must have been a colossal defeat for her. She was no longer in charge of her own house, and the fact that she didn't protest, that she didn't fight back, must have meant that she had already given up on the marriage. When the end came, there were no dramas, no noisy showdowns, no last-minute regrets. The family quietly dispersed. My mother moved to an apartment in the Weequahic section of Newark (taking my sister and me along with her), and my father stayed on alone in the big house, living there until the day he died.

In some perverse way, these events made me extremely happy. I was glad that the truth was finally out in the open, and I welcomed the upheavals and changes that followed as a consequence of that truth. There was something liberating about it, an exhilaration in knowing that the slate had been wiped clean. An entire period of my life had ended, and even as my body continued to go through the motions of finishing up high school and helping my mother move to her new place, my mind had already decamped. Not only was I about to leave home, but home itself had disappeared. There was nothing to return to anymore, nowhere to go but out and away.

I didn't even bother to attend my high school graduation. I offer that as proof, evidence of how little it meant to me. By the time my classmates were donning their caps and gowns and receiving their diplomas, I was already on the other side of the Atlantic. The school had granted me a special dispensation to leave early, and I had booked passage on a student boat that sailed out of New York at the beginning of June. All my savings went into that trip. Birthday money, graduation money, bar mitzvah money, the little bits I'd hoarded from summer jobs—fifteen hundred dollars or so, I can't remember the exact amount. That was the era of Europe on Five Dollars a Day, and if you watched your funds carefully, it was actually possible to do it. I spent over a month in Paris, living in a hotel that cost seven francs a night ($1.40); I traveled to Italy, to Spain, to Ireland. In two and a half months, I lost more than twenty pounds. Everywhere I went, I worked on the novel I had started writing that spring. Mercifully, the manuscript has disappeared, but the story I carried around in my head that summer was no less real to me than the places I went to and the people I crossed paths with. I had some extraordinary encounters, especially in Paris, but more often than not I was alone, at times excessively alone, alone to the point of hearing voices in my head. God knows what to make of that eighteen-year-old boy now. I see myself as a conundrum, the site of inexplicable turmoils, a weightless, wild-eyed sort of creature, slightly touched, perhaps, prone to desperate inner surges, sudden about-faces, swoons, soaring thoughts. If someone approached me in the right way, I could be open, charming, positively gregarious. Otherwise, I was walled off and taciturn, barely present. I believed in myself and yet had no confidence in myself. I was bold and timid, light-footed and clumsy, single-minded and impulsive—a walking, breathing monument to the spirit of contradiction. My life had only just begun, and already I was moving in two directions at once. I didn't know it yet, but in order for me to get anywhere, I was going to have to work twice as hard as anyone else.

The last two weeks of the trip were the strangest. For reasons that had everything to do with James

Joyce and *Ulysses*, I went to Dublin. I had no plans.
My only purpose in going was to be there, and I figured the rest would take care of itself. The tourist
office steered me to a bed-and-breakfast in Donny-
brook, a fifteen-minute bus ride from the center of
town. Besides the elderly couple who ran the place
and two or three of the guests, I scarcely talked to
anyone in all that time. I never even found the courage to set foot in a pub. Somewhere during the course
of my travels, I had developed an ingrown toenail, and
while it sounds like a comical condition, it wasn't the
least bit funny to me. It felt as if the tip of a knife
had been lodged in my big toe. Walking was turned
into a trial, and yet from early in the morning to late
in the afternoon, I did little else but walk, hobbling
around Dublin in my too-tight, disintegrating shoes. I
could live with the pain, I found, but the effort it
called for seemed to drive me ever further into myself,
to erase me as a social being. There was a crotchety
American geezer in full-time residence at the
boardinghouse—a seventy-year-old retiree from Illinois or Indiana—and once he got wind of my
condition, he started filling my head with stories about
how his mother had left an ingrown toenail untended
for years, treating it with patchwork home remedies—
dabs of disinfectant, little balls of cotton—but never
taking the bull by the horns, and wouldn't you know

it, she came down with *cancer of the toe*, which worked its way into her foot, and then into her leg, and then spread through her whole body and eventually did her in. He loved elaborating on the small, gruesome details of his mother's demise (for my own good, of course), and seeing how susceptible I was to what he told me, he never tired of telling the story again. I'm not going to deny that I was affected. A cumbersome annoyance had been turned into a life-threatening scourge, and the longer I delayed taking action, the more dismal my prospects would become. Every time I rode past the Hospital for Incurables on my way into town, I turned my eyes away. I couldn't get the old man's words out of my head. Doom was stalking me, and signs of impending death were everywhere.

Once or twice, I was accompanied on my rambles by a twenty-six-year-old nurse from Toronto. Her name was Pat Gray, and she had checked into the bed-and-breakfast the same evening I had. I fell desperately in love with her, but it was a hopeless infatuation, a lost cause from the start. Not only was I too young for her, and not only was I too shy to declare my feelings, but she was in love with someone else—an Irishman, of course, which explained why she'd come to Dublin in the first place. One night, I recall, she came home from a date with her beloved at around half-past twelve. I was still up at that hour, scribbling away at my novel, and when she saw light coming through the crack under my door, she knocked and asked to come in. I was already in bed, working with a notebook propped against my knees, and she burst in laughing, her cheeks flushed with drink, bubbling over with excitement. Before I could say anything, she threw her arms around my neck and kissed me, and I thought: Miracle of miracles, my dream has come true. But alas, it was only a false alarm. I didn't even have a chance to kiss her back before she was drawing away from me and explaining that her Irishman had proposed to her that night and that she was the happiest girl in the world. It was impossible not to feel glad for her. This straightforward, pretty young woman, with her short hair and innocent eyes and earnest Canadian voice, had chosen me as the person to share the news with. I did my best to congratulate her, to hide my disappointment after that brief, wholly implausible rush of expectation, but the kiss had undone me, had absolutely melted my bones, and it was all I could do not to commit a serious blunder. If I managed to control myself, it was only by turning myself into a block of wood. No doubt a block of wood has good manners, but it's hardly a fitting companion for a celebration.

Everything else was solitude, silence, walking. I read books in Phoenix Park, journeyed out to Joyce's

Martello Tower along the strand, crossed and re-
crossed the Liffey more times than I could count. The
Watts riots took place then, and I remember reading
the headlines at a kiosk on O'Connell Street, but I
also remember a small girl singing with a Salvation
Army band early one evening as people shuffled home
from work—some sad, plaintive song about human
misery and the wonders of God—and that voice is
still inside me, a voice so crystalline as to make the
toughest person fall down and weep, and the remarkable thing about it was that no one paid the slightest
attention to her. The rush-hour crowd rushed past her,
and she just stood on the corner singing her song in
the eerie, dusky, northern light, as oblivious of them
as they were of her, a tiny bird in tattered clothes
chanting her psalm to the broken heart.

Dublin is not a big city, and it didn't take me long
to learn my way around. There was something compulsive about the walks I took, an insatiable urge to
prowl, to drift like a ghost among strangers, and after
two weeks the streets were transformed into something
wholly personal for me, a map of my inner terrain. For
years afterward, every time I closed my eyes before
going to sleep, I was back in Dublin. As wakefulness
dribbled out of me and I descended into semicon-
sciousness, I would find myself there again, walking
through those same streets. I have no explanation for

it. Something important had happened to me there, but I have never been able to pinpoint exactly what it was. Something terrible, I think, some mesmerizing encounter with my own depths, as if in the loneliness of those days I had looked into the darkness and seen myself for the first time.

I started Columbia College in September, and for the next four years the last thing on my mind was money. I worked intermittently at various jobs, but those years were not about making plans, not about preparing for my financial future. They were about books, the war in Vietnam, the struggle to figure out how to do the thing I was proposing to do. If I thought about earning a living at all, it was only in a fitful, haphazard sort of way. At most I imagined some kind of marginal existence for myself—scrounging for crumbs at the far edges of the workaday world, the life of a starving poet.

The jobs I had as an undergraduate were nevertheless instructive. If nothing else, they taught me that my preference for blue-collar work over white-collar work was well founded. At one point in my sophomore year, for example, I was hired by the subdivision of a publishing company to write material for educational filmstrips. I had been subjected to a barrage of "audiovisual aids" during my childhood, and I remembered the intense boredom they invariably produced in me and my friends. It was always a pleasure to leave the classroom and sit in the dark for twenty or thirty minutes (just like going to the movies!), but the clunky images on screen, the monotone voice of the narrator, and the intermittent *ping* that told the teacher when to push the button and move on to the next picture soon took their toll on us. Before long, the room was abuzz with whispered conversations and frantic, half-suppressed giggles. A minute or two later, the spitballs would begin to fly.

I was reluctant to impose this tedium on another generation of kids, but I figured I'd do my best and see if I couldn't put some spark into it. My first day on the job, the supervisor told me to take a look at some of the company's past filmstrips and acquaint myself with the form. I picked out one at random. It was called "Government" or "Introduction to Government," something like that. He set up the spool on a machine and then left me alone to watch the film. About two or three frames into it, I came across a statement that alarmed me. The ancient Greeks had invented the idea of democracy, the text said, accompanied by a painting of bearded men standing around in togas. That was fine, but then it went on to say (*ping*: cut to a painting of the Capitol) that America was a democracy. I turned off the machine, walked down the hall, and knocked on the door of the supervisor's office. "There's a mistake in the filmstrip," I said. "America isn't a democracy. It's a republic. There's a big difference."

He looked at me as if I had just informed him that I was Stalin's grandson. "It's for little children," he said, "not college students. There's no room to go into detail."

"It's not a detail," I answered, "it's an important distinction. In a pure democracy, everyone votes on every issue. We elect representatives to do that for us. I'm not saying that's bad. Pure democracy can be dangerous. The rights of minorities need to be protected, and that's what a republic does for us. It's all spelled out in *The Federalist Papers*. The government has to guard against the tyranny of the majority. Kids should know that."

The conversation became quite heated. I was determined to make my point, to prove that the statement in the filmstrip was wrong, but he refused to swallow it. He pegged me as a troublemaker the instant I opened my mouth, and that was that. Twenty minutes after starting the job, I was given the boot.

Much better was the job I had in the summer after my freshman year—as groundskeeper at the Commodore Hotel in the Catskills. I was hired through the

New York State Employment Agency in midtown Manhattan, a vast government office that found work for the unskilled and the unfortunate, the bottom dogs of society. Humble and badly paid as the position was, at least it offered a chance to get out of the city and escape the heat. My friend Bob Perelman and I signed on together, and the next morning we were dispatched to Monticello, New York, via the Short Line Bus Company. It was the same setup I'd seen three years before, and our fellow passengers were the same bums and down-and-outs I'd rubbed shoulders with during my stint as a summer camp waiter. The only difference was that now I was one of them. The bus fare was deducted from the first paycheck, as was the employment agency's fee, and unless you hung in with the job for some little time, you weren't going to make any money. There were those who didn't like the work and quit after a couple of days. They wound up with nothing—dead broke and a hundred miles from home, feeling they'd been had.

The Commodore was a small, down-at-the-heels Borscht Belt establishment. It was no match for the local competition, the Concord and Grossinger's, and a certain wistfulness and nostalgia hung about the place, a memory of rosier days. Bob and I arrived several weeks in advance of the summer season, and we were responsible for getting the grounds into shape

to welcome an influx of visitors in July and August.
We mowed lawns, clipped bushes, collected trash,
painted walls, repaired screen doors. They gave us a
little hut to live in, a ramshackle box with less square
footage than a beach cabana, and bit by bit we covered the walls of our room with poems—crazy dog-
gerel, filthy limericks, flowery quatrains—laughing
our heads off as we downed endless bottles of Bud-
weiser chug-a-lug beer. We drank the beer because
there was nothing better to do, but given the food we
had to eat, the hops became a necessary component
of our diet as well. There were only a dozen or so
workers on the premises at the time, and they gave us
the low-budget treatment where culinary matters were
concerned. The menu for every lunch and dinner was
the same: Chun King chicken chow mein, straight out
of the can. Thirty years have gone by since then, and
I would still rather go hungry than put another morsel
of that stuff in my mouth.

None of this would be worth mentioning if not for
Casey and Teddy, the two indoor maintenance men I
worked with that summer. Casey and Teddy had been
palling around together for more than ten years, and
by now they were a pair, an indissoluble team, a di-
alectical unit. Everything they did, they did in tan-
dem, traveling from place to place and job to job as
if they were one. They were chums for life, two peas

in a pod, buddies. Not gay, not the least bit interested in each other sexually—but buddies. Casey and Teddy were classic American drifters, latter-day hoboes who seemed to have stepped forth from the pages of a Steinbeck novel, and yet they were so funny together, so full of wisecracks and drunkenness and good cheer, that their company was irresistible. At times they made me think of some forgotten comedy duo, a couple of clowns from the days of vaudeville and silent films. The spirit of Laurel and Hardy had survived in them, but these two weren't bound by the constraints of show business. They were part of the real world, and they performed their act on the stage of life.

Casey was the straight man, Teddy was the card. Casey was thin, Teddy was round. Casey was white, Teddy was black. On their days off they would tramp into town together, drink themselves silly, and then return for their chow mein dinner sporting identical haircuts or dressed in identical shirts. The idea was always to spend all their money in one big binge— and to spend it in exactly the same way, even-steven, penny for penny. The shirts stand out in my mind as a particularly raucous event. They couldn't stop laughing when they showed up in those twin outfits, holding their sides and pointing at each other as if they'd just played an enormous joke on the world.

They were the loudest, ugliest shirts imaginable, a double insult to good taste, and Casey and Teddy were positively seized with mirth as they modeled them for me and Bob. Teddy then shuffled off to the empty ballroom on the ground floor of the main building, sat down at the piano, and launched into what he called his Port Wine Concerto. For the next hour and a half, he clanged forth tuneless improvisations, filling the hall with a tempest of inebriation and noise. Teddy was a man of many gifts, but music was not one of them. Yet there he sat, happy as a clam in the fading light, a Dada maestro at peace with himself and the world.

Teddy had been born in Jamaica, he told me, and had joined the British Navy during World War II. Somewhere along the line, his ship was torpedoed. I don't know how much time elapsed before he was rescued (minutes? hours? days?), but whenever he was found, it was an American ship that found him. From then on he was in the American Navy, he said, and by the end of the war he was an American citizen. It sounded a little fishy to me, but that's the story he told, and who was I to doubt him? In the past twenty years, he seemed to have done everything a man can possibly do, to have run the entire gamut of occupations. Salesman, sidewalk artist in Greenwich Village, bartender, skid row drunk. None of it mattered to him.

A great, rumbling basso laugh accompanied every story he told, and that laugh was like an unending bow to his own ridiculousness, a sign that his only purpose in talking was to poke fun at himself. He made scenes in public places, misbehaved like a willful child, was forever calling people's bluff. It could be exhausting to be with him, but there was also something admirable about the way he caused trouble. It had an almost scientific quality to it, as if he were conducting an experiment, shaking things up for the pure pleasure of seeing where they would land once the dust had settled. Teddy was an anarchist, and because he was also without ambition, because he didn't want the things that other people wanted, he never had to play by anybody's rules but his own.

I have no idea how or where he met Casey. His sidekick was a less flamboyant character than he was, and what I remember best about him was that he had no sense of taste or smell. Casey had been in a barroom fight some years back, had received a knock on the head, and had thenceforth lost all of his olfactory functions. As a result, everything tasted like cardboard to him. Cover his eyes, and he couldn't tell you what he was eating. Chow mein or caviar, potatoes or pudding—there was no difference. Aside from this affliction, Casey was in excellent trim, a feisty welterweight with a New York Irish voice that made him sound like a Dead End Kid. His job was to laugh at Teddy's jokes and make sure his friend didn't take things too far and get himself hauled off to jail. Teddy got close to it one night that summer—standing up in a Monticello restaurant and waving around the menu as he shouted, "I ain't gonna eat this Japanese dog food!"—but Casey calmed him down, and we all managed to finish our meal. I don't suppose it's necessary to add that we weren't in a Japanese restaurant.

By any objective standard, Casey and Teddy were nobodies, a pair of eccentric fools, but they made an unforgettable impression on me, and I have never run across their likes since. That was the reason for going off to work at places like the Commodore Hotel, I think. It's not that I wanted to make a career of it, but those little excursions into the backwaters and shit holes of the world never failed to produce an interesting discovery, to further my education in ways I hadn't expected. Casey and Teddy are a perfect example. I was nineteen years old when I met them, and the things they did that summer are still feeding my imagination today.

In 1967, I signed up for Columbia's Junior Year Abroad Program in Paris. The weeks I'd spent there after finishing high school had whetted my appetite for the place, and I jumped at the chance to go back.

Paris was still Paris, but I was no longer the same person I'd been during my first visit. I had spent the past two years living in a delirium of books, and whole new worlds had been poured into my head, life-altering transfusions had reconstituted my blood. Nearly everything that is still important to me in the way of literature and philosophy I first encountered during those two years. Looking back on that time now, I find it almost impossible to absorb how many books I read. I drank them up in staggering numbers, consumed entire countries and continents of books, could never even begin to get enough of them. Elizabethan playwrights, pre-Socratic philosophers, Russian novelists, Surrealist poets. I read books as if my brain had caught fire, as if my very survival were at stake. One work led to another work, one thought led to another thought, and from one month to the next, I changed my ideas about everything.

The program turned out to be a bitter disappointment. I went to Paris with all sorts of grandiose plans, assuming I would be able to attend any lectures and courses I wanted to (Roland Barthes at the Collège de France, for example), but when I sat down to discuss these possibilities with the director of the program, he flat out told me to forget them. Out of the question, he said. You're required to study French language and grammar, to pass certain tests, to earn so many credits and half-credits, to put in so many class hours here and so many hours there. I found it absurd, a curriculum designed for babies. I'm past all that, I told him. I already know how to speak French. Why go backward? Because, he said, those are the rules, and that's the way it is.

He was so unbending, so contemptuous of me, so ready to interpret my enthusiasm as arrogance and to think I was out to insult him, that we immediately locked horns. I had nothing against the man personally, but he seemed bent on turning our disagreement into a personal conflict. He wanted to belittle me, to crush me with his power, and the longer the conversation went on, the more I felt myself resisting him. At last, a moment came when I'd had enough. All right, I said, if that's the way it is, then I quit. I quit the program, I quit the college, I quit the whole damn thing. And then I got up from my chair, shook his hand, and walked out of the office.

It was a crazy thing to do. The prospect of not getting a B.A. didn't worry me, but turning my back on college meant that I would automatically lose my student deferment. With the troop buildup in Vietnam growing at an alarming rate, I had suddenly put myself in a good position to be drafted into the army. That would have been fine if I supported the war, but I didn't. I was against it, and nothing was ever going to make me fight in it. If they tried to induct me into the army, I would refuse to serve. If they arrested me, I would go to jail.

That was a categorical decision—an absolute, unbudgeable stance. I wasn't going to take part in the war, even if it meant ruining my life.

Still, I went ahead and quit college. I was utterly fearless about it, felt not the slightest tremor of hesitation or doubt, and took the plunge with my eyes wide open. I was expecting to fall hard, but I didn't. Instead, I found myself floating through the air like a feather, and for the next few months I felt as free and happy as I had ever been.

I lived in a small hotel on the rue Clément, directly across from the Marché Saint-Germain, an enclosed market that has long since been torn down. It was an inexpensive but tidy place, several notches up from the fleabag I'd stayed in two years before, and the young couple who ran it were exceedingly kind to me. The man's name was Gaston (stout, small mustache, white shirt, ever-present black apron), and he spent the bulk of his time serving customers in the café on the ground floor, a minuscule hole-in-the-wall that doubled as neighborhood hangout and hotel reception desk. That's where I drank my coffee in the morning, read the newspaper, and became addicted to pinball. I walked a lot during those months, just as I had in Dublin, but I also spent countless hours upstairs in my room, reading and writing. Most of the work I did then has been lost, but I remember writing poems and translating poems, as well as composing a long, exhaustingly complex screenplay for a silent film (part Buster Keaton movie, part philosophical tap dance). On top of all the reading I'd done in the past two years, I had also been going to the movies, primarily at the Thalia and New Yorker theaters, which were no more than a short walk down Broadway from Morningside Heights. The Thalia ran a different double feature every day, and with the price of admission just fifty cents for students, I wound up spending as much time there as I did in the Columbia classrooms. Paris turned out to be an even better town for movies than New York. I became a regular at the Cinémathèque and the Left Bank revival houses, and after a while I got so caught up in this passion that I started toying with the idea of becoming a director. I even went so far as to make some inquiries about attending IDHEC, the Paris film institute, but the application forms proved to be so massive and daunting that I never bothered to fill them out.

When I wasn't in my room or sitting in a movie theater, I was browsing in bookstores, eating in cheap restaurants, getting to know various people, catching a dose of the clap (very painful), and generally exulting in the choice I had made. It would be hard to exaggerate how good I felt during those months. I was at once stimulated and at peace with myself, and though I knew my little paradise would have to end, I did everything I could to prolong it, to put off the hour of reckoning until the last possible moment.

I managed to hold out until mid-November. By the time I returned to New York, the fall semester at Columbia was half over. I assumed there was no chance of being reinstated as a student, but I had promised my family to come back and discuss the matter with the university. They were worried about me, after all, and I figured I owed them that much. Once I had taken care of that chore, I intended to go back to Paris and start looking for a job. Let the draft be damned, I said to myself. If I wound up as a "fugitive from justice," so be it.

None of it worked out as I thought it would. I made an appointment to see one of the deans at Columbia, and this man turned out to be so sympathetic, so fully on my side, that he broke down my defenses within a matter of minutes. No, he said, he didn't think I was being foolish. He understood what I was doing, and he admired the spirit of the enterprise. On the other hand, there was the question of the war, he said. Columbia didn't want to see me go into the army if I didn't want to go, much less wind up in jail for refusing to serve in the army. If I wanted to come back to college, the door was open. I could start attending classes tomorrow, and officially it would be as if I had never missed a day.

How to argue with a man like that? He wasn't some functionary who was just doing his job. He spoke too calmly for that and listened too carefully to what I said, and before long I understood that the only thing in it for him was an honest desire to prevent a twenty-year-old kid from making a mistake, to talk someone out of fucking up his life when he didn't have to. There would be time for that later, n'est-ce pas? He wasn't very old himself—thirty, thirty-five, perhaps—and I still remember his name, even though I never saw him again. Dean Platt. When the university shut down that spring because of the student strike, he quit his job in protest over the administration's handling of the affair. The next thing I heard, he had gone to work for the UN.

The troubles at Columbia lasted from early 1968 until my class graduated the following June. Normal activity all but stopped during that time. The campus became a war zone of demonstrations, sit-ins, and moratoriums. There were riots, police raids, slugfests, and factional splits. Rhetorical excesses abounded, ideological lines were drawn, passions flowed from all sides. Whenever there was a lull, another issue would come up, and the outbursts would begin all over again. In the long run, nothing of any great importance was accomplished. The proposed site for a university gymnasium was changed, a number of academic requirements were dropped, the president resigned and was replaced by another president. That was all. In spite of the efforts of thousands, the ivory tower did not collapse. But still, it tottered for a time, and more than a few of its stones crumbled and fell to the ground.

I took part in some things and kept my distance from others. I helped occupy one of the campus buildings, was roughed up by the cops and spent a night in jail, but mostly I was a bystander, a sympathetic fellow traveler. Much as I would have liked to join in, I found myself temperamentally unfit for group activities. My loner instincts were far too ingrained, and I could never quite bring myself to climb aboard the great ship *Solidarity*. For better or worse, I went on paddling my little canoe—a bit more desperately, perhaps, a bit less sure of where I was going now, but much too stubborn to get out. There probably wouldn't have been time for that anyway. I was steering through rapids, and it took every ounce of my strength just to hold on to the paddle. If I had flinched, there's a good chance I would have drowned.

Some did. Some became casualties of their own righteousness and noble intentions, and the human loss was catastrophic. Ted Gold, one class ahead of me, blew himself to smithereens in a West Village brownstone when the bomb he was building accidentally went off. Mark Rudd, a childhood friend and Columbia dorm neighbor, joined the Weather Underground and lived in hiding for more than a decade. Dave Gilbert, an SDS spokesman whose speeches had impressed me as models of insight and intelligence, is now serving a seventy-five-year prison sentence for his involvement in the Brinks robbery. In the summer of 1969, I walked into a post office in western Massachusetts with a friend who had to mail a letter. As she waited in line, I studied the posters of the FBI's ten most wanted men pinned to the wall. It turned out that I knew seven of them.

That was the climate of my last two years of college. In spite of the distractions and constant turmoil, I managed to do a fair amount of writing, but none of my efforts ever added up to much. I started two novels and abandoned them, wrote several plays I didn't like, worked on poem after poem with largely disappointing results. My ambitions were much greater than my abilities at that point, and I often felt frustrated, dogged by a sense of failure. The only accomplishment I felt proud of was the French poetry I had translated, but that was a secondary pursuit and not even close to what I had in mind. Still, I must not have been totally discouraged. I kept on writing, after all, and when I began publishing articles on books and films in the *Columbia Daily Spectator*, I actually got to see my work in print fairly often. You have to start somewhere, I suppose. I might not have been moving as fast as I wanted to, but at least I was moving. I was up on my feet and walking forward, step by wobbly step, but I still didn't know how to run.

When I look back on those days now, I see myself in fragments. Numerous battles were being fought at the same time, and parts of myself were scattered over a broad field, each one wrestling with a different angel, a different impulse, a different idea of who I was. It sometimes led me to act in ways that were fundamentally out of character. I would turn myself into someone I was not, try wearing another skin for a while, imagine I had reinvented myself. The morose and contemplative stuffed shirt would dematerialize into a fast-talking cynic. The bookish, overly zealous intellectual would suddenly turn around and embrace Harpo Marx as his spiritual father. I can think of several examples of this antic bumbling, but the one that best captures the spirit of the time was a little piece of jabberwocky I contributed to the *Columbia Review*, the undergraduate literary magazine. For reasons that utterly escape me now, I took it upon myself to launch the First Annual Christopher Smart Award. I was a senior then, and the contest rules were published on the last page of the fall issue. I pluck these sentences from the text at random: "The purpose of the award is to give recognition to the great anti-men of our time . . . men of talent who have renounced all worldly ambition, who have turned their backs on the banquet tables of the rich. . . . We have taken Christopher Smart as our model . . . the eighteenth-century Englishman who spurned the easy glory that awaited him as an inventor of rhymed couplets . . . for a life of drunkenness, insanity, religious fanaticism, and prophetic writings. In excess he found his true path, in rejecting the early promise he showed to the academic poets of England, he realized his true greatness. Defamed and ridiculed over the past two centuries, his reputation run through the mud . . . Christopher Smart has been relegated to the sphere of the unknowns. We attempt now, in an age without heroes, to resurrect his name."

The object of the competition was to reward failure. Not common, everyday setbacks and stumbles, but monumental falls, gargantuan acts of self-sabotage. In other words, I wanted to single out the person who had done the least with the most, who had begun with every advantage, every talent, every expectation of worldly success, and had come to nothing. Contestants were asked to write an essay of fifty words or more describing their failure or the failure of someone they knew. The winner would receive a two-volume boxed set of Christopher Smart's *Collected Works*. To no one's surprise but my own, not one entry was submitted.

It was a joke, of course, an exercise in literary leg pulling, but underneath my humorous intentions there was something disturbing, something that was not funny at all. Why the compulsion to sanctify failure? Why the mocking, arrogant tone, the know-it-all posturing? I could be wrong, but it strikes me now that they were an expression of fear—dread of the uncertain future I had prepared for myself—and that my true motive in setting up the contest was to declare myself the winner. The cockeyed, Bedlamite rules were a way of hedging my bets, of ducking the blows that life had in store for me. To lose was to win, to win was to lose, and therefore even if the worst came to pass, I would be able to claim a moral victory. Small comfort, perhaps, but no doubt I was already clutching at straws. Rather than bring my fear out into the open, I buried it under an avalanche of wisecracks and sarcasm. None of it was conscious. I was trying to come to terms with anticipated defeats, hardening myself for the struggles that lay ahead. For the next several years, my favorite sentence in the English language was from the Elizabethan poet Fulke Greville: "I write for those on whom the black ox hath trod."

As it happened, I wound up meeting Christopher Smart. Not the real Christopher Smart, perhaps, but one of his reincarnations, a living example of failed promise and blighted literary fortune. It was the spring of my senior year, just weeks before I was supposed to graduate. Out of nowhere, a man turned up on the Columbia campus and started causing a stir. At first I was only dimly aware of his presence, but little fragments of the stories circulating about him occasionally fell within my earshot. I'd heard that he called himself "Doc," for example, and that for obscure reasons that had something to do with the American economic system and the future of mankind, he was handing out money to strangers, no strings attached. With so many oddball doings in the air back then, I didn't pay much attention.

One night, a couple of my friends talked me into going down to Times Square with them to see the latest Sergio Leone spaghetti western. After the movie let out, we decided to cap off the evening with a little lark and repaired to the Metropole Café at Broadway and Forty-eighth Street. The Metropole had once been a quality jazz club, but now it was a topless go-go bar, complete with wall-to-wall mirrors, strobe lights, and half a dozen girls in glittering G-strings dancing on an elevated platform. We took a table in one of the back corners and started drinking our drinks. Once our eyes had adjusted to the darkness, one of my friends spotted "Doc" sitting alone in the opposite corner of the room. My friend went over and asked him to join us, and when the bearded, somewhat disheveled mystery man sat down beside me, mumbling something about Gene Krupa and what the hell had happened to this place, I turned my eyes away from the dancers for a moment and shook hands with the legendary, forgotten novelist, H. L. Humes.

He had been one of the founders of the *Paris Review* back in the fifties, had published two successful early books (*The Underground City* and *Men Die*), and then, just as he was beginning to make a name for himself, had vanished from sight. He just dropped off the literary map and was never heard from again.

I don't know the full story, but the bits and pieces I heard from him suggested that he'd had a rough time of it, had endured a long run of reversals and miseries. Shock treatments were mentioned, a ruined marriage, several stays in mental hospitals. By his own account,

he'd been forced to stop writing for physical reasons—
not by choice. The electroshock therapy had damaged
his system, he said, and every time he picked up a
pen, his legs would start to swell up, causing him
unbearable pain. With the written word no longer
available to him, he now had to rely on talk to get his
"message" across to the world. That night, he gave a
full-scale demonstration of how thoroughly he had
mastered this new medium. First in the topless bar,
and then on a nearly seventy-block walk up Broadway
to Morningside Heights, the man talked a blue streak,
rattling and rambling and chewing our ears off with a
monologue that resembled nothing I had ever heard
before. It was the rant of a hipster-visionary-
neoprophet, a relentless, impassioned outflow of par-
anoia and brilliance, a careening mental journey that
bounced from fact to metaphor to speculation with
such speed and unpredictability that one was left
dumbfounded, unable to say a word. He had come to
New York on a mission, he told us. There were fifteen
thousand dollars in his pocket, and if his theories
about finance and the structures of capitalism were
correct, he would be able to use that money to bring
down the American government.

It was all quite simple, really. His father had just
died, leaving Doc the aforementioned sum as an in-
heritance, and rather than squander the money on

himself, our friend was proposing to give it away. Not
in a lump, and not to any particular charity or person,
but to everyone, to the whole world all at once. To
that end he had gone to the bank, cashed the check,
and converted it into a stack of fifty-dollar bills. With
those three hundred portraits of Ulysses S. Grant as
his calling cards, he was going to introduce himself
to his coconspirators and unleash the greatest economic revolution in history. Money is a fiction, after
all, worthless paper that acquires value only because
large numbers of people choose to give it value. The
system runs on faith. Not truth or reality, but collec-
tive belief. And what would happen if that faith were
undermined, if large numbers of people suddenly began to doubt the system? Theoretically, the system
would collapse. That, in a nutshell, was the object of
Doc's experiment. The fifty-dollar bills he handed out
to strangers weren't just gifts; they were weapons in
the fight to make a better world. He wanted to set an
example with his profligacy, to prove that one could
disenchant oneself and break the spell that money
held over our minds. Each time he disbursed another
chunk of cash, he would instruct the recipient to
spend it as fast as he could. Spend it, give it away,
get it circulating, he would say, and tell the next person to do the same. Overnight, a chain reaction would
be set in motion, and before you knew it, so many

fifties would be flying through the air that the system would start to go haywire. Waves would be emitted, neutron charges from thousands, even millions of different sources would bounce around the room like little rubber balls. Once they built up enough speed and momentum, they would take on the strength of bullets, and the walls would begin to crack.

I can't say to what degree he actually believed this. Deranged as he might have been, a man of his intelligence surely would have known a stupid idea when he heard it. He never came out and said so, but deep down I think he understood what drivel it was. That didn't stop him from enjoying it, of course, and from spouting off about his plan at every opportunity, but it was more in the spirit of a wacko performance piece than a genuine political act. H. L. Humes wasn't some crackpot schizo taking orders from Martian command center. He was a ravaged, burnt-out writer who had run aground on the shoals of his own consciousness, and rather than give up and renounce life altogether, he had manufactured this little farce to boost his morale. The money gave him an audience again, and as long as people were watching, he was inspired, manic, the original one-man band. He pranced about like a buffoon, turning cartwheels and jumping through flames and shooting himself out of cannons, and from all I could gather, he loved every minute of it.

As he marched up Broadway that night with me and my friends, he put on a spectacular show. Between the cascading words and the barks of laughter and the jags of cosmological music, he would wheel around and start addressing strangers, breaking off in midsentence to slap another fifty-dollar bill in someone's hand and urge him to spend it like there was no tomorrow. Rambunctiousness took control of the street that night, and Doc was the prime attraction, the pied piper of mayhem. It was impossible not to get caught up in it, and I must admit that I found his performance highly entertaining. However, just as we neared the end of our journey and I was about to go home, I made a serious blunder. It must have been one or two in the morning by then. Somewhere off to my right, I heard Doc muttering to himself. "Any of you cats got a place to crash?" he said, and because he sounded so cool and nonchalant, so profoundly indifferent to the matters of this world, I didn't think twice about it. "Sure," I said, "you can sleep on my couch if you want to." Needless to say, he accepted my invitation. Needless to say, I had no idea what I had gotten myself into.

It's not that I didn't like him, and it's not that we didn't get along. For the first couple of days, in fact, things went rather smoothly. Doc planted himself on the couch and rarely stirred, rarely even brought the soles of his feet into contact with the floor. Aside from an occasional trip to the bathroom, he did nothing but sit, eat pizza, smoke marijuana, and talk. I bought the pizza for him (with his money), and after telling him five or six times that I wasn't interested in dope, he finally got the message and stopped offering it to me. The talk was incessant, however, the same repertoire of addled riffs he'd unfurled on the first night, but his arguments were more ample now, more fleshed out, more focused. Hours would go by, and his mouth never stopped moving. Even when I got up and left the room, he would go on talking, delivering his ideas to the wall, the ceiling, the light fixtures, and scarcely even notice that I was gone.

There wouldn't have been a problem if the place had been a little larger. The apartment had just two rooms and a kitchen, and since my bedroom was too small to hold anything but a bed, my work table was set up in the living room—which also happened to be where the couch was. With Doc permanently installed on the couch, it was all but impossible for me to get any work done. The spring semester was drawing to a close, and I had a number of term papers to write in order to complete my courses and graduate, but for the first two days I didn't even bother to try. I figured that I had a little margin and therefore didn't panic. Doc would be leaving soon, and once I had my desk

back, I would be able to get down to work. By the
morning of the third day, however, I realized that my
houseguest had no intention of leaving. It wasn't that
he was overstaying his welcome on purpose; the
thought of leaving simply hadn't entered his head.
What was I supposed to do? I didn't have the heart
to kick him out. I already felt too sorry for him, and
I couldn't find the courage to take such a drastic step.

The next few days were exceedingly difficult. I did
what I could to cope, to see if some minor adjustments
could improve the situation. In the end, things might
have panned out—I don't know—but three or four
days after I put Doc in the bedroom and took over the
living room for myself, disaster struck. It happened
on one of the most beautiful Sundays I can remember,
and it was no one's fault but my own. A friend called
to invite me to play in an outdoor basketball game,
and rather than leave Doc alone in the apartment, I
took him along with me. Everything went well. I
played in the game and he sat by the side of the court,
listening to the radio and yakking to himself or my
friends, depending on whether anyone was within
range. As we were returning home that evening, however, someone spotted us on the street. "Aha," this
person said to me, "so that's where he's been hiding."
I had never particularly liked this person, and when
I told him to keep Doc's whereabouts under his hat,

I realized that I might just as well have been talking to a lamppost. Sure enough, the buzzer of my apartment started ringing early the next morning. The campus celebrity had been found, and after his mysterious weeklong absence, H. L. Humes was more than happy to indulge his followers. All day long, groups of nineteen- and twenty-year-olds tramped into my apartment to sit on the floor and listen to Doc impart his skewed wisdom to them. He was the philosopher king, the metaphysical pasha, the bohemian holy man who saw through the lies their professors had taught them, and they couldn't get enough of it.

I was deeply pissed off. My apartment had been turned into a twenty-four-hour meeting hall, and much as I would have liked to hold Doc responsible for it, I knew that he wasn't to blame. His acolytes had come of their own accord, without invitations or appointments, and once the crowds began to gather, I could no more ask him to turn them away than I could ask the sun to stop shining. Talk was what he lived for. It was his final barrier against oblivion, and because those kids were there with him now, because they sat at his feet and hung on his every word, he could temporarily delude himself into thinking that all was not lost for him. I had no problem with that. For all I cared, he could go on talking until the next century. I just didn't want him doing it in my apartment.

Torn between compassion and disgust, I came up with a coward's compromise. It happened during one of the rare lulls of that period, at a moment when no unannounced visitors were in the apartment. I told Doc that he could stay—and that I would clear out instead. I had piles of work to do, I explained, and rather than dump him on the street before he'd found another place to live, I would go to my mother's apartment in Newark and write my school papers. In exactly one week I would return, and when I came back I expected him to be gone. Doc listened carefully as I outlined this plan to him. When I had finished, I asked him if he understood. "I dig, man," he said, speaking in his calmest, most gravelly jazzman's voice, "it's cool," and that was all there was to it. We went on to talk about other things, and somewhere in the course of our conversation that night he mentioned that many years back, as a young man in Paris, he had occasionally played chess with Tristan Tzara. This is one of the few concrete facts that has stayed with me. Over time, nearly everything else I heard from the mouth of H. L. Humes has disappeared. I can remember what his voice sounded like, but very little of what he said. All those great verbal marathons, those forced marches to the hinterlands of reason, those countless hours of listening to him unravel his plots and conspiracies and secret correspondences—

all that has been reduced to a blur. The words are no more than a buzzing in my brain now, an unintelligible swarm of nothingness.

The next morning, as I was packing my bag and getting ready to leave, he tried to give me money. I turned him down, but he kept insisting, peeling off fifties from his wad like some racetrack gambler, telling me to take it, that I was a good kid, that we had to "share the wealth," and in the end I caved in to the pressure and accepted three hundred dollars from him. I felt terrible about it then and still feel terrible about it now. I had wanted to stay above that business, to resist taking part in the pathetic game he was playing, and yet when my principles were finally put on the line, I succumbed to temptation and allowed greed to get the better of me. Three hundred dollars was a large sum in 1969, and the lure of that money turned out to be stronger than I was. I put the bills in my pocket, shook Doc's hand good-bye, and hurried out of the apartment. When I returned a week later, the place was neat as a pin, and there was no sign of him anywhere. Doc had left, just as he had promised he would.

I saw him only once more after that. It was about a year later, and I was riding uptown on the number 4 bus. Just as we made the turn onto 110th Street, I spotted him through the window—standing on the corner of Fifth Avenue and the northern edge of Central Park. He appeared to be in bad shape. His clothes were rumpled, he looked dirty, and his eyes had a lost, vacant expression that had not been there before. He's slipped into hard drugs, I said to myself. Then the bus moved on, and I lost sight of him. Over the next days and weeks, I kept expecting to see him again, but I never did. Twenty-five years went by, and then, just five or six months ago, I opened *The New York Times* and stumbled across a small article on the obituary page announcing that he was dead.

Little by little, I learned how to improvise, trained myself to roll with the punches. During my last two years at Columbia, I took any number of odd freelance jobs, gradually developing a taste for the kind of literary hackwork that would keep me going until I was thirty—and which ultimately led to my downfall. There was a certain romance in it, I suppose, a need to affirm myself as an outsider and prove that I could make it on my own without kowtowing to anyone else's idea of what constituted the good life. My life would be good if and only if I stuck to my guns and refused to give in. Art was holy, and to follow its call meant making any sacrifice that was demanded of you, maintaining your purity of purpose to the bitter end.

Knowing French helped. It was hardly a rarefied skill, but I was good enough at it to have some translation jobs tossed my way. Art writings, for example, and an exceptionally tedious document from the French Embassy about the reorganization of its staff that droned on for more than a hundred pages. I also tutored a high school girl one spring, traveling across town every Saturday morning to talk to her about poetry, and another time I was collared by a friend (for no pay) to stand on an outdoor podium with Jean Genet and translate his speech in defense of the Black Panthers. Genet walked around with a red flower tucked behind his ear and rarely stopped smiling the whole time he was on the Columbia campus. New York seemed to make him happy, and he handled the attention he received that day with great poise. One night not long after that, I bumped into an acquaintance in the West End, the old student watering hole at Broadway and 114th Street. He told me that he had just started working for a pornography publisher, and if I wanted to try my hand at writing a dirty book, the price was fifteen hundred dollars per novel. I was more than willing to have a go at it, but my inspiration petered out after twenty or thirty pages. There were just so many ways to describe that one thing, I discovered, and my stock of synonyms soon dried up. I started writing book reviews instead—for a shoddily put together publication aimed at students. Sensing that the magazine wasn't going to add up to much, I signed my articles with a pseudonym, just to keep things interesting. Quinn was the name I chose for myself, Paul Quinn. The pay, I remember, was twenty-five dollars per review.

When the results of the draft lottery were announced at the end of 1969, I lucked out with number 297. A blind draw of the cards saved my skin, and the nightmare I had been girding myself against for several years suddenly evaporated. Who to thank for that unexpected mercy? I had been spared immense amounts of pain and trouble, had literally been given back control of my life, and the sense of relief was incalculable. Jail was no longer in the picture for me. The horizon was clear on all sides, and I was free to walk off in any direction I chose. As long as I traveled light, there was nothing to stop me from going as far as my legs would take me.

That I wound up working on an oil tanker for several months was largely a matter of chance. You can't work on a ship without a Merchant Seaman's card, and you can't obtain a Merchant Seaman's card without a job on a ship. Unless you know someone who can break through the circle for you, it's impossible to get in. The someone who did it for me was my mother's second husband, Norman Schiff. My mother had remarried about a year after her divorce from my father, and by 1970 my stepfather and I had been fast friends for nearly five years. An excellent man with a generous heart, he had consistently stood behind me and supported my vague, impractical ambitions. His early death in 1982 (at age fifty-five) remains one of the great sorrows of my life, but back then as I was finishing up my year of graduate work and preparing to leave school, his health was still reasonably good. He practiced law, mostly as a labor negotiator, and among his many clients at the time was the Esso Seaman's Union, for which he worked as legal counsel. That was how the idea got planted in my head. I asked him if he could swing me a job on one of the Esso tankers, and he said he would handle it. And without further ado, that was precisely what he did.

There was a lot of paperwork to take care of, trips to the union hall in Belleville, New Jersey, physical exams in Manhattan, and then an indefinite period of waiting until a slot opened up on one of the ships coming into the New York area. In the meantime, I took a temporary job with the United States Census Bureau, collecting data for the 1970 census in Harlem. The work consisted of climbing up and down staircases in dimly lit tenement buildings, knocking on apartment doors, and helping people fill out the government forms. Not everyone wanted to be helped, of course, and more than a few were suspicious of the white college boy prowling around their hallways, but enough people welcomed me in to make me feel that I wasn't completely wasting my time. I stayed with it for approximately a month, and then—sooner than I was expecting—the ship called.

I happened to be sitting in a dentist's chair at that moment, about to have a wisdom tooth pulled. Every morning since my name had gone on the list, I had checked in with my stepfather to let him know where I could be reached that day, and he was the one who tracked me down at the dentist's office. The timing couldn't have been more comical. The Novocain had already been injected into my gums, and the dentist had just picked up the pliers and was about to attack my rotten tooth when the receptionist walked in and announced that I was wanted on the phone. Extremely urgent. I climbed out of the chair with the bib still tied around my neck, and the next thing I knew, Norman was telling me that I had three hours to pack and get myself aboard the S.S. *Esso Florence* in Elizabeth, New Jersey. I stammered my apologies to the dentist and hightailed it out of there.

The tooth stayed in my mouth for another week. When it finally came out, I was in Baytown, Texas.

The *Esso Florence* was one of the oldest tankers in the fleet, a pip-squeak relic from a bygone age. Put a two-door Chevy next to a stretch limousine, and you'll have some idea of how it compared to the supertankers they build today. Already in service during World War II, my ship had logged untold thousands of watery miles by the time I set foot on it. There were enough beds on board to accommodate a hundred men, but only thirty-three of us were needed to take care of the work that had to be done. That meant that each person had his own room—an enormous benefit when you considered how much time we had to spend together. With other jobs you get to go home at night, but we were boxed in with each other twenty-four hours a day. Every time you looked up, the same faces were there. We worked together, lived together, and ate together, and without the chance for some genuine privacy, the routine would have been intolerable.

We shuttled between the Atlantic coast and the Gulf of Mexico, loading and unloading airplane fuel at various refineries along the way: Charleston, South Carolina; Tampa, Florida; Galveston, Texas. My initial responsibilities were mopping floors and making beds, first for the crew and then for the officers. The technical term for the position was "utilityman," but in plain language the job was a combination of janitor, garbage collector, and chambermaid. I can't say that I was thrilled to be scrubbing toilets and picking up dirty socks, but once I got the hang of it, the work turned out to be incredibly easy. In less than a week, I had polished my custodial skills to such a point that it took me only two or two and a half hours to finish my chores for the day. That left me with abundant quantities of free time, most of which I spent alone in my room. I read books, I wrote, I did everything I had done before—but more productively, somehow, with better powers of concentration now that there was so little to distract me. In many ways, it felt like an almost ideal existence, a perfect life.

Then, after a month or two of this blissful regimen, I was "bumped." The ship rarely traveled more than five days between ports, and nearly everywhere we docked some crew members would get off and others would get on. The jobs for the fresh arrivals were doled out according to seniority. It was a strict pecking order, and the longer you had worked for the company, the more say you had in what you were given. As low man on the totem pole, I had no say at all. If an old-timer wanted my job, he had only to ask for it, and it was his. After my long run of good luck, the boom finally fell on me somewhere in Texas. My replacement was a man named Elmer, a bovine Fundamentalist bachelor who happened to be the longest-serving, most famous utilityman of them all. What I had been able to do in two hours, Elmer now did in six. He was the slowest of the slow, a smug and untalkative mental lightweight who waddled about the ship in a world of his own, utterly ignored by the other crew members, and in all my experience I have never met a person who ate as much as he did. Elmer could pack away mountains of food—two, three, and four helpings at every meal—but what made it fascinating to watch him was not so much the scope of his appetite as the way he went about satisfying it: daintily, fastidiously, with a compulsive sense of decorum. The best part was the cleanup operation at the end. Once Elmer had eaten his fill, he would spread his napkin on the table before him and begin patting and smoothing the flimsy paper with his hands, slowly transforming it into a flat square. Then he would fold the napkin into precise longitudinal sections, methodically halving the area until it had been divided into eighths. In the end, the square would be turned into a long, rectilinear strip with all four edges exactly aligned. At that point, Elmer would carefully take hold of the edges, raise the napkin to his lips, and begin to rub. The action was all in the head: a slow back-and-forth swiveling that went on for twenty or thirty seconds. From start to finish, Elmer's hands never stirred. They would be fixed in the air as his large head turned left, right, and left again, and through it all his eyes never betrayed the slightest thought or emotion. The Cleaning of the Lips was a dogged, mechanical procedure, an act of ritual purification. Cleanliness is next to godliness, Elmer once told me. To see him with that napkin, you understood that he was doing God's work.

I was able to observe Elmer's eating habits at such close range because I had been bumped into the galley. The job of messman quadrupled my hours and made my life altogether more eventful. My responsibilities now included serving three meals a day to the crew (about twenty men), washing dishes by hand, cleaning the mess hall, and writing out the menus for the steward, who was generally too drunk to bother with them himself. My breaks were short—no more than an hour or two between meals—and yet in spite of having to work much harder than before, my income actually shrank. On the old job, there had been plenty of time for me to put in an extra hour or two in the evenings, scraping and painting in the boiler room, for example, or refurbishing rusty spots on deck, and those volunteer jobs had padded my paycheck quite nicely. Still, in spite of the disadvantages, I found working in the mess hall more of a challenge than mopping floors had been. It was a public job, so to speak, and in addition to all the hustling around that was now required of me, I had to stay on my toes as far as the men were concerned. That, finally, was my most important task: to learn how to handle the griping and rough-tempered complaints, to fend off insults, to give as good as I got.

Elmer aside, the crew was a fairly grimy, ill-mannered bunch. Most of the men lived in Texas and Louisiana, and apart from a handful of Chicanos, one or two blacks, and the odd foreigner who cropped up now and then, the dominant tone on board was white, redneck, and blue collar. A jocular atmosphere prevailed, replete with funny stories and dirty jokes and much talk about guns and cars, but there were deep, smoldering currents of racism in many of those men, and I made a point of choosing my friends carefully. To hear one of your coworkers defend South African apartheid as you sat with him over a cup of coffee ("they know how to treat niggers down there") doesn't bring much joy to the soul, and if I found myself hanging out mostly with the dark-skinned and Spanish-speaking men around me, there was a good reason for it. As a New York Jew with a college degree, I was an entirely alien specimen on that ship, a man from Mars. It would have been easy to make up stories about myself, but I had no interest in doing that. If someone asked me what my religion was or where I came from, I told him. If he didn't like it, I figured that was his problem. I wasn't going to hide who I was or pretend to be someone else just to avoid trouble. As it happened, I had only one awkward run-in the whole time I was there. One of the men started calling me Sammy whenever I walked by. He seemed to think it was funny, but as I failed to see any humor in the epithet, I told him to stop it. He did it again the next day, and once again I told him to stop it. When he did it again the day after that, I understood that polite words were not going to be enough. I grabbed hold of his shirt, slammed him against the wall, and very calmly told him that if he ever called me that again, I would kill him. It shocked me to hear myself talk like that. I was not someone who trafficked in violence, and I had never made that kind of threat to anyone, but for that one brief instant, a demon took possession of my soul. Luckily, my willingness to fight was enough to defuse the fight before it began. My tormentor threw up his hands in a gesture of peace. "It was just a joke," he said, "just a joke," and that was the end of it. As time went on, we actually became friends.

I loved being out on the water, surrounded by nothing but sky and light, the immensity of the vacant air. Seagulls accompanied us wherever we went, circling overhead as they waited for buckets of garbage to be dumped overboard. Hour after hour, they would hover patiently just above the ship, scarcely beating their wings until the scraps went flying, at which point they would plunge frantically into the foam, calling out to each other like drunks at a football game. Few pleasures can match the spectacle of that foam, of sitting at the stern of a large ship and staring into the white, churning tumult of the wake below. There is something hypnotic about it, and on still days the sense of well-being that washes through you can be overpowering. On the other hand, rough weather also holds its charms. As summer melted away and we headed into autumn, the inclemencies multiplied, bringing down some wild winds and pelting rains, and at those moments the ship felt no more safe or solid than a child's paper boat. Tankers have been known to crack in half, and all it takes is one wrong wave to do the job. The worst stretch, I remember, occurred when we were off Cape Hatteras in late September or early October, a twelve- or fifteen-hour period of flipping and flopping through a tropical storm. The captain stayed at the wheel all night, and even after the worst of it was over and the steward instructed me to carry the captain his breakfast the next morning, I was nearly blown overboard when I stepped onto the bridge with my tray. The rain might have stopped, but the wind speed was still at gale force.

For all that, working on the *Esso Florence* had

little to do with high-seas adventure. The tanker was essentially a floating factory, and rather than introduce me to some exotic, swashbuckling life, it taught me to think of myself as an industrial laborer. I was one of millions now, an insect toiling beside countless other insects, and every task I performed was part of the great, grinding enterprise of American capitalism. Petroleum was the primary source of wealth, the raw material that fueled the profit machine and kept it running, and I was glad to be where I was, grateful to have landed in the belly of the beast. The refineries where we loaded and unloaded our cargo were enormous, hellish structures, labyrinthine networks of hissing pipes and towers of flame, and to walk through one of them at night was to feel that you were living in your own worst dream. Most of all, I will never forget the fish, the hundreds of dead, iridescent fish floating on the rank, oil-saturated water around the refinery docks. That was the standard welcoming committee, the sight that greeted us every time the tugboats pulled us into another port. The ugliness was so universal, so deeply connected to the business of making money and the power that money bestowed on the ones who made it—even to the point of disfiguring the landscape, of turning the natural world inside out—that I began to develop a grudging respect for it. Get to the bottom of things, I told myself, and this was how the world looked. Whatever you might think of it, this ugliness was the truth.

Whenever we docked somewhere, I made it my business to leave the ship and spend some time ashore. I had never been south of the Mason-Dixon line, and those brief jaunts onto solid ground took me to places that felt a lot less familiar or understandable than anything I'd met up with in Paris or Dublin. The South was a different country, a separate American universe from the one I'd known in the North. Most of the time, I tagged along with one or two of my shipmates, going the rounds with them as they visited their customary haunts. If Baytown, Texas, stands out with particular clarity, that is because we spent more time there than anywhere else. I found it a sad, crumbling little place. Along the main drag, a row of once elegant movie theaters had been turned into Baptist churches, and instead of announcing the titles of the latest Hollywood films, the marquees now sported fiery quotations from the Bible. More often than not, we wound up in sailors' bars on the back streets of broken-down neighborhoods. All of them were essentially the same: squalid, low-life joints; dim drinking holes; dank corners of oblivion. Everything was always bare inside. Not a single picture on the walls, not one touch of publican warmth. At most there was a quarter-a-rack pool table, a jukebox stuffed with country-and-western songs, and a drink menu that consisted of just one drink: beer.

Once, when the ship was in a Houston dry dock for some minor repairs, I spent the afternoon in a skid row bar with a Danish oiler named Freddy, a wild man who laughed at the slightest provocation and spoke English with an accent so thick that I scarcely understood a word he said. Walking down the street in the blinding Texas sun, we crossed paths with a drunken couple. It was still early in the day, but this man and woman were already so soused, so entrenched in their inebriation, they must have been going at the booze since dawn. They wobbled along the sidewalk with their arms around each other, listing this way and that, their heads lolling, their knees buckling, and yet both with enough energy left to be engaged in a nasty, foul-mouthed quarrel. From the sound of their voices, I gathered they'd been at it for years—a pair of bickering stumblebums in search of their next drink, forever repeating the same lines to each other, forever shuffling through the same old song and dance. As it turned out, they wound up in the same bar where Freddy and I chose to while away the afternoon, and because I was not more than ten feet away from them, I was in a perfect position to observe the following little drama:

The man leaned forward and barked out at the

woman across the table. "Darlene," he said, in a drawling, besotted voice, "get me another beer."

Darlene had been nodding off just then, and it took her a good long moment to open her eyes and bring the man into focus. Another long moment ticked by, and then she finally said, "What?"

"Get me a beer," the man repeated. "On the double."

Darlene was waking up now, and a lovely, fuck-you sassiness suddenly brightened her face. She was clearly in no mood to be pushed around. "Get it yourself, Charlie," she snapped back at him. "I ain't your slave, you know."

"Damn it, woman," Charlie said. "You're my wife, ain't you? What the hell did I marry you for? Get me the goddamn beer!"

Darlene let out a loud, histrionic sigh. You could tell she was up to something, but her intentions were still obscure. "Okay, darling," she said, putting on the voice of a meek, simpering wife, "I'll get it for you," and then stood up from the table and staggered over to the bar.

Charlie sat there with a grin on his face, gloating over his small, manly victory. He was the boss, all right, and no one was going to tell him different. If you wanted to know who wore the pants in that family, just talk to him.

A minute later, Darlene returned to the table with a fresh bottle of Bud. "Here's your beer, Charlie," she said, and then, with one quick flick of the wrist, proceeded to dump the contents of the bottle onto her husband's head. Bubbles foamed up in his hair and eyebrows; rivulets of amber liquid streamed down his face. Charlie made a lunge for her, but he was too drunk to get very close. Darlene threw her head back and burst out laughing. "How do you like your beer, Charlie?" she said. "How do you like your fucking beer?"

Of all the scenes I witnessed in those bars, nothing quite matched the bleak comedy of Charlie's baptism, but for overall oddness, a plunge into the deepest heart of the grotesque, I would have to single out Big Mary's Place in Tampa, Florida. This was a large, brightly lit emporium that catered to the whims of dockhands and sailors, and it had been in business for many years. Among its features were half a dozen pool tables, a long mahogany bar, inordinately high ceilings, and live entertainment in the form of quasi-naked go-go dancers. These girls were the cornerstone of the operation, the element that set Big Mary's Place apart from other establishments of its kind—and one look told you that they weren't hired for their beauty, nor for their ability to dance. The sole criterion was size. The bigger the better was how Big Mary put it, and the bigger you got, the more money you were paid. The effect was quite disturbing. It was a freak show of flesh, a cavalcade of bouncing white blubber, and with four girls dancing on the platform behind the bar at once, the act resembled a casting call for the lead role in *Moby Dick*. Each girl was a continent unto herself, a mass of quivering lard decked out in a string bikini, and as one shift replaced another, the assault on the eyes was unrelenting. I have no memory of how I got there, but I distinctly recall that my companions that night were two of the gentler souls from the ship (Martinez, a family man from Texas, and Donnie, a seventeen-year-old boy from Baton Rouge) and that they were both just as flummoxed as I was. I can still see them sitting across from me with their mouths hanging open, doing everything they could not to laugh from embarrassment. At one point, Big Mary herself came over and sat down with us at our table. A splendid dirigible of a woman dressed in an orange pants suit and wearing a ring on every finger, she wanted to know if we were having a good time. When we assured her that we were, she waved to one of the girls at the bar. "Barbara," she yelled, belting out the word in a brassy, three-pack-a-day voice, "get your fat butt over here!" Barbara came, all smiles and good humor, laughing as Big Mary poked her in the stomach and pinched the ample rolls bulging from her hips. "She was a scrawny one at first," Mary explained, "but I've fattened her up pretty good. Ain't that so, Barbara?" she said, cackling like some mad scientist who's just pulled off a successful experiment, and Barbara couldn't have agreed with her more. As I listened to them talk, it suddenly occurred to me that I had it all wrong. I hadn't gone to sea. I'd run off and joined the circus.

Another friend was Jeffrey, the second cook (a.k.a. breakfast chef), from Bogalusa, Louisiana. We happened to have been born on the same day, and apart from the near-infant Donnie, we were the youngest members of the crew. It was the first time out for both of us, and since we worked together in the galley, we got to know each other reasonably well. Jeffrey was one of life's winners—a bright, handsome, fun-loving ladies' man with a taste for flashy clothes—and yet very practical and ambitious, a down-to-earth schemer who was quite consciously using his job on the ship to learn the ins and outs of cooking. He had no intention of making a career out of oil tankers, no desire to turn himself into an old salt. His dream was to become a chef in a high-class restaurant, maybe even to own that restaurant himself, and if nothing unexpected rose up to stop him, I don't doubt that that's exactly what he's doing today. We couldn't have been more unlike, Jeffrey and I, but we got along comfortably with each other. It was only natural that we should sometimes go ashore together when the ship was in port, but because Jeffrey was black, and because he had spent his whole life in the South, he knew that many of the places I went to with white crew members were off-limits to him. He made that perfectly clear to me the first time we planned an outing. "If you want me to go with you," he said, "you'll have to go where I can go." I tried to convince him that he could go anywhere he pleased, but Jeffrey wasn't buying the argument. "Maybe up North," he said. "Down here it's different." I didn't force the issue. When I went out for beers with Jeffrey, we drank them in black bars instead of white bars. Except for the skin color of the clientele, the atmosphere was the same.

One night in Houston, Jeffrey talked me into going to a dance club with him. I never danced and never went to clubs, but the thought of spending a few hours in a place that wasn't a low-rent dive tempted me, and I decided to take my chances. The club turned out to be a splashy disco hall thronged with hundreds of young people, the hottest black nightspot in town. There was a live band onstage, psychedelic strobe lights bouncing off the walls, hard liquor available at the bar. Everything pulsed with sex and chaos and loud music. It was Saturday night fever, Texas style.

Jeffrey was dressed to the teeth, and within four minutes he struck up a conversation with one of the many stunning girls floating around the bar, and four minutes after that they were out on the dance floor together, lost in an ocean of bodies. I sat down at a table and sipped my drink, the only white person in the building. No one gave me any trouble, but I got some odd, penetrating looks from a number of people, and by the time I finished my bourbon, I understood that I should be shoving off. I phoned for a cab and then went outside to wait in the parking lot. When the driver showed up a few minutes later, he started cursing. "Goddammit," he said. "Goddammit to hell. If I'd known you were calling from here, I wouldn't have come." "Why not?" I asked. "Because this is the worst fucking place in Houston," he said. "They've had six murders here in the past month. Every damn weekend, somebody else gets shot."

In the end, the months I spent on that ship felt like years. Time passes in a different way when you're out on the water, and given that the bulk of what I experienced was utterly new to me, and given that I was constantly on my guard because of that, I managed to crowd an astonishing number of impressions

and memories into a relatively small sliver of my life.
Even now, I don't fully understand what I was hoping
to prove by shipping out like that. To keep myself off
balance, I suppose. Or, very simply, just to see if I
could do it, to see if I could hold my own in a world
I didn't belong to. In that respect, I don't think I
failed. I can't say what I accomplished during those
months, but at the same time I'm certain I didn't fail.

I received my discharge papers in Charleston.
The company provided airfare home, but you could
pocket the money if you wanted to and make your own
travel arrangements. I chose to keep the money. The
trip by milk train took twenty-four hours, and I rode
back with a fellow crew member from New York, Juan
Castillo. Juan was in his late forties or early fifties, a
squat, lumpy man with a big head and a face that
looked like something pieced together with the skins
and pulps of nineteen mashed potatoes. He had just
walked off an oil tanker for the last time, and in ap-
preciation of his twenty-five years of service to the
company, Esso had given him a gold watch. I don't
know how many times Juan pulled that watch out of
his pocket and looked at it during the long ride home,
but every time he did, he would shake his head for a
few seconds and then burst out laughing. At one point,
the ticket collector stopped to talk to us during one
of his strolls down the aisle of the car. He looked very

natty in his uniform, I remember, a black Southern gentleman of the old school. In a haughty, somewhat condescending manner, he opened the conversation by asking: "You boys going up North to work in the steel mills?"

We must have been a curious pair, Juan and I. I recall that I was wearing a beat-up leather jacket at the time, but other than that I can't see myself, have no sense of what I looked like or what other people saw when they looked at me. The ticket collector's question is the only clue I have. Juan had taken pictures of his shipmates to put in the family album at home, and I remember standing on the deck and looking into the camera for him as he clicked the shutter. He promised to send me a copy of the photo, but he never did.

I toyed with the idea of going out for another run on an Esso tanker, but in the end I decided against it. My salary was still being sent to me through the mail (for every two days I'd been on the ship, I received one day's pay on land), and my bank account was beginning to look fairly robust. For the past few months, I had been slowly coming to the conclusion that my next step should be to leave the country and live abroad for a while. I was willing to ship out again if necessary, but I wondered if I hadn't built up a large enough stake already. The three or four thousand dollars I'd earned from the tanker struck me as a sufficient sum to get started with, and so rather than continue in the merchant marine, I abruptly shifted course and began plotting a move to Paris.

France was a logical choice, but I don't think I went there for logical reasons. That I spoke French, that I had been translating French poetry, that I knew and cared about a number of people who lived in France—surely those things entered into my decision, but they were not determining factors. What made me want to go, I think, was the memory of what had happened to me in Paris three years earlier. I still hadn't gotten it out of my system, and because that visit had been cut short, because I had left on the assumption that I would soon be returning, I had walked around with a feeling of unfinished business, of not having had my fill. The only thing I wanted just then was to hunker down and write. By recapturing the inwardness and freedom of that earlier time, I felt that I would be putting myself in the best possible position to do that. I had no intention of becoming an expatriate. Giving up America was not part of the plan, and at no time did I think I wouldn't return. I just needed a little breathing room, a chance to figure out, once and for all, if I was truly the person I thought I was.

What comes back to me most vividly from my last weeks in New York is the farewell conversation I had with Joe Reilly, a homeless man who used to hang around the lobby of my apartment building on West 107th Street. The building was a run-down, nine-story affair, and like most places on the Upper West Side, it housed a motley collection of people. With no effort at all, I can summon forth a fair number of them, even after a quarter of a century. The Puerto Rican mailman, for example, and the Chinese waiter, and the fat blonde opera singer with the Lhasa apso. Not to mention the black homosexual fashion designer with his black fur coat and the quarreling clarinetists whose vicious spats would seep through the walls of my apartment and poison my nights. On the ground floor of this gray brick building, one of the apartments had been divided down the middle, and each half was occupied by a man confined to a wheelchair. One of them worked at the news kiosk on the corner of Broadway and 110th Street; the other was a retired rabbi. The rabbi was a particularly charming fellow, with a pointy artist's goatee and an ever-present black beret, which he wore at a rakish, debonair angle. On most days, he would wheel himself out of his apartment and spend some time in the lobby, chatting with Arthur, the superintendent, or with various tenants getting in and out of the elevator. Once, as I entered the building, I caught sight of him through the glass door in his usual spot, talking to a bum in a long, dark overcoat. It struck me as an odd conjunction, but from the way the bum stood there and from the tilt of the rabbi's head, it was clear that they knew each other well. The bum was an authentic down-and-outer, a scab-faced wino with filthy clothes and cuts dotting his half-bald scalp, a scrofulous wreck of a man who appeared to have just crawled out of a storm drain. Then, as I pushed open the door and stepped into the lobby, I heard him speak. Accompanied by wild, theatrical gestures—a sweep of the left arm, a finger darting from his right hand and pointing to the sky—a sentence came booming out of him, a string of words so unlikely and unexpected that at first I didn't believe my ears. "It was no mere fly-by-night acquaintance!" he said, rolling each syllable of that florid, literary phrase off his tongue with such relish, such blowhard bravura, such magnificent pomposity, that he sounded like some tragic ham delivering a line from a Victorian melodrama. It was pure W. C. Fields—but several octaves lower, with the voice more firmly in control of the effects it was striving to create. W. C. Fields mixed with Ralph Richardson, perhaps, with a touch of barroom bombast thrown in for good measure. However you wanted to define it, I had never heard a voice do what that voice did.

When I walked over to say hello to the rabbi, he introduced me to his friend, and that was how I learned the name of that singular gentleman, that mightiest of fallen characters, the one and only Joe Reilly.

According to the rabbi, who filled me in on the story later, Joe had started out in life as the privileged son of a wealthy New York family, and in his prime he had owned an art gallery on Madison Avenue. That was when the rabbi had met him—back in the old days, before Joe's disintegration and collapse. The rabbi had already left the pulpit by then and was running a music publishing company. Joe's male lover was a composer, and as the rabbi happened to publish that man's work, in the natural course of things he and Joe crossed paths. Then, very suddenly, the lover died. Joe had always had a drinking problem, the rabbi said, but now he hit the bottle in earnest, and his life began to fall apart. He lost his gallery; his family turned its back on him; his friends walked away. Little by little, he sank into the gutter, the last hole at the bottom of the world, and in the rabbi's opinion he would never climb out again. As far as he was concerned, Joe was a hopeless case.

Whenever Joe came around after that, I would dig into my pocket and hand him a few coins. What moved me about these encounters was that he never let his mask drop. Blustering forth his thanks in the highly embroidered, Dickensian language that came so effortlessly to him, he would assure me that I would be paid back promptly, just as soon as circumstances allowed. "I am most grateful to you for this bounty, young man," he would say, "most grateful indeed. It's just a loan, of course, so you needn't fret about being reimbursed. As you might or might not know, I've suffered some small setbacks lately, and this generosity of yours will go a long way towards helping me back to my feet." The sums in question were never more than a pittance—forty cents here, twenty-five cents there, whatever I happened to be carrying around with me—but Joe never flagged in his enthusiasm, never once let on that he realized what an abject figure he was. There he stood, dressed in a circus clown's rags, his unwashed body emitting the foulest of stinks, and still he persisted in keeping up his pose as a man of the world, a dandy temporarily down on his luck. The pride and self-deception that went into this act were both comical and heartbreaking, and every time I went through the ritual of giving him another handout, I had trouble keeping my balance. I never knew whether to laugh or cry, whether to admire him or shower him with pity. "Let me see, young man," he would continue, studying the coins I had just put in his palm. "I have, let's see, I have here in my hand, hmmm, fifty-five cents. Add that to the eighty cents you gave me that last time, and then add that, hmmm, add that to the forty cents you gave me the time before that, and it turns out that I owe you a grand total of, hmmm, let's see, a grand total of . . . one dollar and fifteen cents." Such was Joe's arithmetic. He just plucked figures out of thin air and hoped they sounded good. "No problem, Joe," I would say. "A dollar and fifteen cents. You'll give it to me the next time."

When I came back to New York from the Esso ship, he seemed to be floundering, to have lost some ground. He looked more bruised to me, and the old panache had given way to a new heaviness of spirit, a whining, tearful sort of despair. One afternoon, he broke down in front of me as he recounted how he had been beaten up in some alleyway the night before. "They stole my books," he said. "Can you imagine that? The animals stole my books!" Another time, in the middle of a snowstorm, as I left my ninth-floor apartment and walked to the elevator down the hall, I found him sitting alone on the staircase, his head buried in his hands.

"Joe," I said, "are you all right?"

He lifted his head. His eyes were infused with sorrow, misery, and defeat. "No, young man," he said. "I'm not all right, not the least bit all right."

"Is there anything I can do for you?" I asked. "You look terrible, just terrible."

"Yes," he said, "now that you mention it, there is one thing you can do for me," and at that point he suddenly reached out and took hold of my hand. Then, looking me straight in the eye, he gathered up his strength and said, in a voice trembling with emotion, "You can take me back into your apartment, lie down on the bed, and let me make love to you."

The bluntness of his request took me completely by surprise. I had been thinking more along the lines of a cup of coffee or a bowl of soup. "I can't do that," I said. "I like women, Joe, not men. Sorry, but I don't do that kind of thing."

What he said next lingers in my mind as one of the best and most pungent statements I have ever heard. Without wasting a second, and without the slightest trace of disappointment or regret, he dismissed my answer with a shrug of the shoulders and said, in a buoyant, ringing tone of voice, "Well, you asked me—and I told you."

I left for Paris some time in the middle of February 1971. After that encounter on the staircase, I didn't see Joe again for several weeks. Then, just days before my departure, I bumped into him on Broadway. He was looking much better, and the hangdog look had disappeared from his face. When I told him I was about to move to Paris, he was off and running again, as effusive and full of himself as ever. "It's odd that you should mention Paris," he said. "Indeed, it's a most timely coincidence. Not two or three days ago, I happened to be walking down Fifth Avenue, and who should I bump into but my old friend Antoine, director of the Cunard Lines. 'Joe,' he said to me, 'Joe, you're not looking too well,' and I said, 'No, Antoine, it's true, I haven't been at my best lately,' and Antoine said that he wanted to do something for me, lend a helping hand, so to speak, and put me back on track. What he proposed, right there on Fifth Avenue the other day, was to sail me over to Paris on one of his ships and put me up at the Hôtel Georges V. All expenses paid, of course, with a new wardrobe thrown into the bargain. He said I could stay there as long as I liked. Two weeks, two months, even two years if I wanted. If I decide to go, which I think I will, I'll be leaving before the end of the month. Which means, young man, that we'll be in Paris at the same time. A pleasant prospect, no? Expect to see me there. We'll have tea, dinner. Just leave a message for me at the hotel. On the Champs-Elysées. That's where we'll meet next, my friend. In Paris, on the Champs-

Elysées." And then, bidding me farewell, he shook my hand and wished me a safe and happy voyage.

I never saw Joe Reilly again. Even before we said good-bye that day, I knew that I was talking to him for the last time, and when he finally disappeared into the crowd a few minutes later, it was as if he had already turned into a ghost. All during the years I lived in Paris, I thought of him every time I set foot on the Champs-Elysées. Even now, whenever I go back there, I still do.

My money didn't last as long as I thought it would. I found an apartment within a week of my arrival, and once I had shelled out for the agency commission, the security deposit, the gas and electric service, the first month's rent, the last month's rent, and the state-mandated insurance policy, I didn't have much left. Right from the start, therefore, I had to scramble to keep my head above water. In the three and a half years I lived in France, I had any number of jobs, bounced from one part-time gig to another, freelanced until I was blue in the face. When I didn't have work, I was looking for work. When I had work, I was thinking about how to find more. Even at the best of times, I rarely earned enough to feel secure, and yet in spite of one or two close calls, I managed to avoid total

ruin. It was, as they say, a hand-to-mouth existence.
Through it all, I wrote steadily, and if much of what
I wrote was discarded (mostly prose), a fair chunk of
it (mostly poems and translations) was not. For better
or worse, by the time I returned to New York in July
1974, the idea of not writing was inconceivable to me.

Most of the work I landed came through friends
or the friends of friends or the friends of friends of
friends. Living in a foreign country restricts your op-
portunities, and unless you know some people who are
willing to help you, it is next to impossible to get
started. Not only will doors not open when you knock
on them, but you won't even know where to look for
those doors in the first place. I was lucky enough to
have some allies, and at one time or another they all
moved small mountains on my behalf. Jacques Dupin,
for example, a poet whose work I had been translating
for several years, turned out to be director of
publications at the Galerie Maeght, one of the leading
art galleries in Europe. Among the painters and sculp-
tors shown there were Miró, Giacometti, Chagall, and
Calder, to mention just a few. Through Jacques's in-
tervention, I was hired to translate several art books
and catalogues, and by my second year in Paris, when
my funds were perilously close to bottoming out, he
saved the situation by giving me a room to live in—
free of charge. These acts of kindness were essential,

and I can't imagine how I would have survived without them.

At one point, I was steered to the Paris bureau of *The New York Times*. I can't remember who was responsible for the connection, but an editor named Josette Lazar began throwing translations my way whenever she could: articles for the Sunday *Book Review*, op-ed pieces by Sartre and Foucault, this and that. One summer, when my money was at low ebb again, she finagled a position for me as the nighttime switchboard operator at the *Times* office. The phone didn't ring very often, and mostly I just sat at a desk, working on poems or reading books. One night, however, there was a frantic call from a reporter stationed somewhere in Europe. "Sinyavsky's defected," she said. "What should I do?" I had no idea what she should do, but since none of the editors was around at that hour, I figured I had to tell her something. "Follow the story," I said. "Go where you have to go, do what you have to do, but stick with the story, come hell or high water." She thanked me profusely for the advice and then hung up.

Some jobs started out as one thing and ended up as another, like a botched stew you can't stop tinkering with. Just stir in some additional ingredients and see if it doesn't taste better. A good example would be my little adventure among the North Vietnamese in Paris, which began with an innocent phone call from Mary McCarthy to my friend André du Bouchet. She asked him if he knew of anyone who could translate poetry from French into English, and when he gave her my name, she called and invited me to her apartment to discuss the project. It was early 1973, and the war in Vietnam was still dragging on. Mary McCarthy had been writing about the war for several years, and I had read most of her articles, which I found to be among the best pieces of journalism published at the time. In the course of her work, she had come in contact with many Vietnamese from both the northern and southern halves of the country. One of them, a professor of literature, was putting together an anthology of Vietnamese poetry, and she had offered to help arrange for an English-language version to be published in America. The poems had already been translated into French, and the idea was to translate those translations into English. That was how my name had come up, and that was why she wanted to talk to me.

In her private life, Mary McCarthy was Mrs. West. Her husband was a well-to-do American businessman, and their Paris apartment was a large, richly appointed place filled with art objects, antiques, and fine furniture. Lunch was served to us by a maid in a black and white uniform. A china bell sat on the table next to my hostess's right hand, and every time she picked it up and gave it a little shake, the maid would return to the dining room to receive further instructions. There was an impressive, *grande dame* quality to the way Mary McCarthy handled these domestic protocols, but the truth was that she turned out to be everything I had hoped she would be: sharp-witted, friendly, unpretentious. We talked about many things that afternoon, and by the time I left her apartment several hours later, I was loaded down with six or seven books of Vietnamese poetry. The first step was for me to familiarize myself with their contents. After that, the professor and I would meet and get down to work on the anthology.

I read the books and enjoyed them, particularly *The Book of Kieu*, the national epic poem. The details escape me now, but I remember becoming interested in some of the formal problems presented by traditional Vietnamese verse structures, which have no equivalents in Western poetry. I was happy to have been offered the job. Not only was I going to be paid well, but it looked as if I might learn something into the bargain. A week or so after our lunch, however, Mary McCarthy called to tell me that there had been an emergency, and her professor friend had gone back to Hanoi. She wasn't sure when he would be returning to Paris, but for the time being at least, the project had been put on hold.

Such were the breaks. I pushed the books aside and hoped the job wasn't dead, even though I knew it was. Several days went by, and then, out of the blue, I received a telephone call from a Vietnamese woman living in Paris. "Professor So-and-so gave us your name," she said. "He told us you can translate into English. Is that true?" "Yes," I said, "it's true." "Good," she said. "We have a job for you."

The job turned out to be a translation of the new North Vietnamese constitution. I had no qualms about doing the work, but I found it strange that they should have come to me. You would think that a document of that sort would be translated by someone in the government—directly from Vietnamese into English, and not from French, and if from French, not by an enemy American living in Paris. I didn't ask any questions, however. I still had my fingers crossed about the anthology and didn't want to ruin my chances, so I accepted the job. The following evening, the woman came to my apartment to drop off the manuscript. She was a biologist in her mid-thirties—thin, unadorned, exceptionally reserved in her manner. She didn't say anything about a fee for the work, and from her silence I gathered that there wasn't going to be one. Given the tangled political nuances of the situation (the war between our two countries, my feelings about that war, and so on), I was hardly disposed to press her about money. Instead, I began asking her questions about the Vietnamese poems I had been reading. At one point, I got her to sit down at my desk with me and draw a diagram that explained the traditional verse forms that had piqued my curiosity. Her sketch proved to be very helpful, but when I asked her if I could keep it for future reference, she shook her head, crumpled up the paper, and put it in her pocket. I was so startled, I didn't say a word. In that one small gesture, an entire world had been revealed to me, an underground universe of fear and betrayal in which even a scrap of paper was suspect. Trust no one; cover your tracks; destroy the evidence. It wasn't that she was afraid of what I might do with the diagram. She was simply acting out of habit, and I couldn't help feeling sorry for her, sorry for both of us. It meant that the war was everywhere, that the war had tainted everything.

The constitution was eight or ten pages long, and apart from some standard Marxist-Leninist phrases ("running dogs of imperialism," "bourgeois lackeys"), it was pretty dry stuff. I did the translation the next day, and when I called my biologist friend to tell her that the work was finished, she sounded inordinately

pleased and grateful. It was only then that she told
me about my payment: an invitation to dinner. "By
way of thanks," as she put it. The restaurant happened
to be in the Fifth Arrondissement, not far from where
I lived, and I had eaten there several times before. It
was the simplest and cheapest Vietnamese restaurant
in Paris, but also the best. The only ornament in the
place was a black-and-white photograph of Ho Chi
Minh hanging on the wall.

Other jobs were entirely straightforward, the es-
sence of simplicity: tutoring a high school boy in English, serving as simultaneous translator at a small
international conference of Jewish scholars (dinner included), translating material by and about Giacometti
for the art critic David Sylvester. Few of these jobs
paid well, but they all brought in something, and if I
didn't always have great stocks of food in my refrigerator, I was rarely without a pack of cigarettes in my
pocket. Still, I couldn't have sustained myself on odds
and ends alone. They helped to keep me going, but
add them all together, and they wouldn't have been
enough to live on for more than a few weeks, a few
months at most. I needed another source of income to
pay the bills, and as luck would have it, I found one.
To put it more accurately, it found me. For the first
two years I spent in Paris, it was the difference between eating and not eating.

The story goes back to 1967. During my earlier stay as a student, an American friend had introduced me to a woman I will call Madame X. Her husband, Monsieur X, was a well-known film producer of the old style (epics, extravaganzas, a maker of deals), and it was through her that I started working for him. The first opportunity arose just a few months after I arrived. There was no telephone in the apartment I had rented, which was still the case with many Paris apartments in 1971, and there were only two ways of contacting me: by *pneumatique*, a rapid intracity telegram sent through the post office, or by coming to the apartment and knocking on the door. One morning, not long after I had woken up, Madame X knocked on the door. "How would you like to earn a hundred dollars today?" she said. The job seemed simple enough: read a movie script, then write out a six- or seven-page summary. The only constraint was time. A potential backer of the film was waiting on a yacht somewhere in the Mediterranean, and the outline had to be delivered to him within forty-eight hours.

Madame X was a flamboyant, stormy character, the first larger-than-life woman I had ever met. Mexican by birth, married since the age of eighteen or nineteen, the mother of a boy just a few years younger than I was, she lived her own independent life, drifting in and out of her husband's orbit in ways I was

still too unsophisticated to understand. Artistic by
temperament, she dabbled by turns at painting and
writing, showing talent in both fields but with too little
discipline or concentration to take those talents very
far. Her true gift was encouraging others, and she surrounded herself with artists and would-be artists of all
ages, hobnobbing with the known and the unknown
as both a colleague and a patroness. Wherever she
went, she was the center of attention, the gorgeous,
soulful woman with the long black hair and the
hooded cloaks and the clattering Mexican jewelry—
moody, generous, loyal, her head full of dreams.
Somehow or other, I had made it onto her list, and
because I was young and just starting out, she counted
me among those friends who needed looking after, the
poor and struggling ones who required an occasional
helping hand.

There were others too, of course, and a couple of
them were invited along with me that morning to earn
the same round figure that I had been promised. A
hundred dollars sounds like pocket change today, but
back then it represented more than half a month's
rent, and I was in no position to turn down a sum of
that magnitude. The work was to be done at the X's'
apartment, an immense, palatial establishment in the
Sixteenth Arrondissement with untold numbers of
high-ceilinged rooms. The starting time was set for

eleven o'clock, and I showed up with half an hour to spare.

I had met each of my coworkers before. One of them was an American in his mid-twenties, a fey unemployed pianist who walked around in women's high heels and had recently spent time in a hospital with a collapsed lung. The other was a Frenchman with decades of film experience, mostly as a second-unit director. Among his credits were the chariot scenes in *Ben-Hur* and the desert scenes in *Lawrence of Arabia*, but since those days of wealth and success, he had fallen on hard times: nervous breakdowns, periods of confinement in mental wards, no work. He and the pianist were major reclamation projects for Madame X, and throwing me together with them was just one example of how she operated. No matter how good her intentions were, they were invariably undermined by complex, impractical schemes, a desire to kill too many birds with a single stone. Rescuing one person is hard enough, but to think you can save the whole world at once is to ask for disappointment.

So there we were, the most mismatched trio ever assembled, gathered around the gigantic table in the dining room of the X's's gigantic apartment. The script in question was also gigantic. A work of nearly three hundred pages (three times the length of the normal script), it looked like the telephone book of a large city. Because the Frenchman was the only one with any professional knowledge of the movies, the pianist and I deferred to him and allowed him to take charge of the discussion. The first thing he did was pull out a sheet of blank paper and begin jotting down the names of actors. Frank Sinatra, Dean Martin, Sammy Davis, Jr., followed by six or seven others. When he was finished, he slapped his hands on the table with great satisfaction. "You see this piece of paper?" he asked. The pianist and I nodded our heads. "Believe it or not, this little piece of paper is worth ten million dollars." He patted the list once or twice and then pushed it aside. "Ten, maybe twelve million dollars." He spoke with the utmost conviction, betraying not the slightest hint of humor or irony. After a brief pause, he opened the manuscript to the first page. "Well," he said, "are we ready to begin?"

Almost immediately, he became excited. On the second or third line of the first page, he noticed that the name of one of the characters began with the letter Z. "Aha!" he said. "Z. This is very important. Pay close attention, my friends. This is going to be a political film. Mark my words."

Z was the title of a film by Costa-Gavras, a popular hit two years earlier. That film had most assuredly been about politics, but the screenplay we had been asked to summarize was not. It was an action thriller about smuggling. Largely set in the Sahara Desert, it featured trucks, motorcycles, several gangs of warring bad guys, and a number of spectacular explosions. The only thing that set it apart from a thousand other movies was its length.

We had been at work for approximately a minute and a half, and already the pianist had lost interest. He stared down at the table and snickered to himself as the Frenchman rambled on, lurching from one bit of nonsense to another. Suddenly, without any transition or preamble, the poor man started talking about David Lean, recalling several philosophical discussions he'd had with the director fifteen years earlier. Then, just as abruptly, he broke off from his reminiscences, stood up from the table, and walked around the room, straightening the pictures on the walls. When he was finished with that task, he announced that he was going to the kitchen to look for a cup of coffee. The pianist shrugged. "I think I'll go play the piano," he said, and just like that, he was gone as well.

As I waited for them to return, I started reading the script. I couldn't think of anything else to do, and by the time it dawned on me that neither one of them would be coming back, I had worked my way through most of it. Eventually, one of Monsieur X's associates drifted into the room. He was a youngish, good-natured American who also happened to be Madame X's special friend (the complexities of the household were fathomless), and he instructed me to finish the job on my own, guaranteeing that if I managed to produce an acceptable piece of work by seven o'clock, all three of the hundred-dollar payments would be mine. I told him I would do my best. Before I hustled out of there and went home to my typewriter, he gave me an excellent bit of advice. "Just remember," he said. "This is the movies, not Shakespeare. Make it as vulgar as you can."

I wound up writing the synopsis in the extravagant, overheated language of Hollywood coming attractions. If they wanted vulgar, I would give them vulgar. I had sat through enough movie trailers to know what they sounded like, and by dredging up every hackneyed phrase I could think of, by piling one excess on top of another, I boiled the story down to seven pages of frantic, nonstop action, a bloodbath wrought in pulsing, Technicolor prose. I finished typing at six-thirty. An hour later, a chauffeur-driven car arrived downstairs to take me and my girlfriend to the restaurant where Madame and Monsieur X had invited us for dinner. The moment we got there, I was supposed to deliver the pages to him in person.

Monsieur X was a small, enigmatic man in his mid to late fifties. Of Russian-Jewish origin, he spoke

several languages with equal fluency, often shifting
from French to English to Spanish in the course of a
single conversation, but always with the same cumbersome accent, as if in the end he didn't feel at home
in any of them. He had been producing movies for
over thirty years, and in a career of countless ups and
downs, he had backed good films and bad films, big
films and small films, art films and trash films. Some
had made piles of money for him, others had put him
miserably in debt. I had crossed paths with him only
a few times before that night, but he had always struck
me as a lugubrious person, a man who played things
close to the vest—shrewd, hidden, unknowable. Even
as he talked to you, you sensed that he was thinking
about something else, working out some mysterious
calculations that might or might not have had anything
to do with what he was saying. It's not that they didn't,
but at the same time it would have been wrong to
assume that they did.

That night in the restaurant, he was noticeably
edgy when I arrived. A potentially lucrative deal
hinged on the work of one of his wife's arty friends,
and he was anything but optimistic. I had barely settled into my seat when he asked to see the pages I
had written. As the rest of us made small talk around
the table, Monsieur X sat hunched in silence, reading
through my florid, slam-bang paragraphs. Little by lit-

tle, a smile began to form on his lips. He started nodding to himself as he turned the pages, and once or twice he was even heard to mutter the word "good" under his breath. He didn't look up, however. Not until he'd come to the last sentence did he finally raise his head and give me the verdict.

"Excellent," he said. "This is just what I wanted." The relief in his voice was almost palpable.

Madame X said something about how she'd told him so, and he confessed that he'd had his doubts. "I thought it would be too literary," he said. "But this is good. This is just right."

He became very effusive after that. We were in a large, gaudy restaurant in Montmartre, and he immediately started snapping his fingers for the flower girl. She came scurrying over to our table, and Monsieur X bought a dozen roses, which he handed to my girlfriend as an impromptu gift. Then he reached into his breast pocket, pulled out his checkbook, and wrote me a check for three hundred dollars. It was the first check I had ever seen from a Swiss bank.

I was glad to have delivered the goods under pressure, glad to have earned my three hundred bucks, glad to have been roped into the absurd events of that day, but once we left the restaurant and I returned to my apartment on the rue Jacques Mawas, I assumed that the story was over. It never once crossed my mind that Monsieur X might have further plans for me. One afternoon the following week, however, as I sat at my table working on a poem, I was interrupted by a loud knock on the door. It was one of Monsieur X's gofers, an elderly gentleman I'd seen lurking about the house on my visits there but had never had the pleasure of talking to. He wasted no time in getting to the point. Are you Paul Auster? he asked. When I told him I was, he informed me that Monsieur X wanted to see me. When? I asked. Right now, he said. There's a taxi waiting downstairs.

It was a little like being arrested by the secret police. I suppose I could have refused the invitation, but the cloak-and-dagger atmosphere made me curious, and I decided to go along to see what was up. In the cab, I asked my chaperon why I had been summoned like this, but the old man merely shrugged. Monsieur X had told him to bring me back to the house, and that was what he was doing. His job was to follow orders, not ask questions. I therefore remained in the dark, and as I mulled over the question myself, the only answer I could think of was that Monsieur X was no longer satisfied with the work I had done for him. By the time I walked into his apartment, I was fully expecting him to ask me for the money back.

He was dressed in a paisley smoking jacket with

satin lapels, and as he entered the room where I'd been told to wait for him, I noticed that he was rubbing his hands together. I had no idea what that gesture meant.

"Last week," he said, "you do good works for me. Now I want to make package deal."

That explained the hands. It was the gesture of a man ready to do business, and all of a sudden, on the strength of that dashed-off, tongue-in-cheek manuscript I'd concocted for him the other day, it looked as though I was about to be in business with Monsieur X. He had at least two jobs for me right away, and if all went well with those, the implication was that others would follow. I needed the money and accepted, but not without a certain wariness. I was stepping into a realm I didn't understand, and unless I kept my wits about me, I realized that strange things could be in store for me. I don't know how or why I knew that, but I did. When Monsieur X started talking about giving me a role in one of his upcoming movies, a swashbuckling adventure story for which I would need fencing and riding lessons, I held my ground. "We'll see," I said. "The fact is, I'm not much interested in acting."

Apparently, the man on the yacht had liked my synopsis just as much as Monsieur X had. Now he wanted to take things to the next level and was commissioning a translation of the screenplay from French into English. That was the first job. The second job was somewhat less cut-and-dried. Madame X was at work on a play, Monsieur X told me, and he had agreed to finance a production at the Round House Theatre in London next season. The piece was about Quetzalcoatl, the mythical plumed serpent, and since much of it was written in verse, and since much of that verse was written in Spanish, he wanted me to turn it into English and make sure that the drama was in playable shape. Fine, I said, and that was how we left it. I did both jobs, everyone was satisfied, and two or three months later, Madame X's play was performed in London. It was a vanity production, of course, but the reviews were good, and all in all the play was quite well received. A British publisher happened to attend one of the performances, and he was so impressed by what he'd seen that he proposed to Madame X that she turn the play into a prose narrative, which he would then publish as a book.

That was where things started getting sticky between me and Monsieur X. Madame X didn't have it in her to write the book on her own, and he believed that I was the one person on earth capable of helping her. I might have accepted the job under different circumstances, but since he also wanted me to go to Mexico to do the work, I told him I wasn't interested.

Why the book had to be written in Mexico was never made clear to me. Research, local color, something along those lines, I'm not sure. I was fond of Madame X, but being thrown together with her for an unspecified length of time struck me as less than a good idea. I didn't even have to think about Monsieur X's offer. I turned him down on the spot, figuring that would close the matter once and for all. Events proved me wrong. True indifference has power, I learned, and my refusal to take the job irritated Monsieur X and got under his skin. He wasn't in the habit of having people say no to him, and he became hell-bent on changing my mind. Over the next several months, he launched an all-out campaign to wear down my resistance, besieging me with letters, telegrams, and promises of ever greater sums of money. In the end, I reluctantly gave in. As with every other bad decision I've made in my life, I acted against my better judgment, allowing secondary considerations to interfere with the clarity of my instincts. In this case, what tipped the balance was money. I was having a hard time of it just then, desperately falling behind in my struggle to remain solvent, and Monsieur X's offer had grown so large, would eliminate so many of my problems at once, that I talked myself into accepting the wisdom of compromise. I thought I was being clever. Once I had climbed down from my high horse, I laid out my conditions in the toughest terms I could think of. I would go to Mexico for exactly one month, I told him—no more, no less—and I wanted full payment in cash before I left Paris. It was the first time I had ever negotiated for anything, but I was determined to protect myself, and I refused to yield on any of these points. Monsieur X was less than thrilled with my intractability, but he understood that I'd gone as far as I would go and gave in to my demands. The same day I left for Mexico, I deposited twenty-five one-hundred-dollar bills in my bank account. Whatever happened in the next month, at least I wouldn't be broke when I returned.

I was expecting things to go wrong, but not quite to the degree that they did. Without rehashing the whole complicated business (the man who threatened to kill me, the schizophrenic girl who thought I was a Hindu god, the drunken, suicidal misery that per-meated every household I entered), the thirty days I spent in Mexico were among the grimmest, most un-settling days of my life. Madame X had already been there for a couple of weeks when I arrived, and I quickly learned that she was in no shape to work on the book. Her boyfriend had just left her, and this love drama had plunged her into the throes of an acute despair. It's not that I blamed her for her feelings, but she was so distraught, so distracted by her suffering, that the book was the last thing she wanted to think about. What was I supposed to do? I tried to get her started, tried to make her sit down with me and discuss the project, but she simply wasn't interested. Every time we took a stab at it, the conversation would quickly veer off onto other subjects. Again and again, she broke down and cried. Again and again, we got nowhere. After several of these attempts, I understood that the only reason she was bothering to make an effort was because of me. She knew that I was being paid to help her, and she didn't want to let me down, didn't want to admit that I had come all this way for nothing.

That was the essential flaw in the arrangement. To assume that a book can be written by a person who is not a writer is already a murky proposition, but granting that such a thing is possible, and granting that the person who wants to write the book has someone else to help with the writing of it, perhaps the two of them, with much hard work and dedication, can arrive at an acceptable result. On the other hand, if the person who is not a writer does not want to write a book, of what use is the someone else? Such was the quandary I found myself in. I was willing to help Madame X write her book, but I couldn't help her unless she wanted to write it, and if she didn't want to, there was nothing I could do but sit around and wait until she did.

So there I sat, biding my time in the little village of Tepotzolán, hoping that Madame X would wake up one morning and discover that she had a new outlook on life. I was staying with Madame X's brother (whose unhappy marriage to an American woman was on its last legs), and I filled my days with aimless walks around the dusty town, stepping over mangy dogs, batting flies out of my face, and accepting invitations to drink beers with the local drunks. My room was in a stucco outbuilding on the brother's property, and I slept under muslin netting to guard against the tarantulas and mosquitoes. The crazy girl kept showing up with one of her friends, a Central American Hare Krishna with a shaved head and orange robes, and boredom ate away at me like some tropical disease. I wrote one or two short poems, but otherwise I languished, unable to think, bogged down by a persistent, nameless anxiety. Even the news from the outside world was bad. An earthquake killed thousands of people in Nicaragua, and my favorite baseball player, Roberto Clemente, the most elegant and electrifying performer of his generation, went down in a small plane that was trying to deliver emergency relief to the victims. If anything pleasant stands out from the miasma and stupor of that month, it would be the hours I spent in Cuernavaca, the radiant little city that Malcolm Lowry wrote about in *Under the Volcano*. There, quite by chance, I was introduced to a man who was described to me as the last living descendant of Montezuma. A tall, stately gent of around sixty, he had impeccable manners and wore a silk ascot around his neck.

When I finally returned to Paris, Monsieur X arranged to meet me in the lobby of a hotel on the Champs-Elysées. Not the Hôtel Georges V, but another one directly across the street. I can't remember why he chose that place, but I think it had something to do with an appointment he'd scheduled there before mine, strictly a matter of convenience. In any case, we didn't talk in the hotel. The instant I showed up, he led me outside again and pointed to his car, which was waiting for us just in front of the entrance. It was a tan Jaguar with leather upholstery, and the man behind the wheel was dressed in a white shirt. "We'll talk in there," Monsieur X said. "It's more private." We climbed into the back seat, the driver started up the engine, and the car pulled away from the curb. "Just drive around," Monsieur X said to the chauffeur. I suddenly felt as if I had landed in a gangster movie.

Most of the story was known by then, but he

wanted me to give him a full report, an autopsy of the
failure. I did my best to describe what had happened,
expressing more than once how sorry I was that things
hadn't worked out, but with Madame X's heart no
longer in the book, I said, there wasn't much I could
do to motivate her. Monsieur X seemed to accept all
this with great calm. As far as I could tell, he wasn't
angry, not even especially disappointed. Just when I
thought the interview was about to end, however, he
brought up the subject of my payment. Since nothing
had been accomplished, he said, it seemed only right
that I should give him back the money, didn't it? No,
I said, it didn't seem right at all. A deal is a deal,
and I had gone to Mexico in good faith and had kept
up my end of the bargain. No one had ever suggested
that I write the book *for* Madame X. I was supposed
to write it *with* her, and if she didn't want to do the
work, it wasn't my job to force her to do it. That was
precisely why I'd asked for the money in advance. I
was afraid that something like this would happen, and
I needed to know that I would be paid for my time—
no matter how things turned out.

He saw the logic of my argument, but that didn't
mean he was willing to back down. All right, he said,
keep the money, but if you want to go on working for
me, you'll have to do some more jobs to square the
account. In other words, instead of asking me to return

the money in cash, he wanted me to give it back in labor. I told him that was unacceptable. Our account was square, I said, I wasn't in debt to him, and if he wanted to hire me for other jobs, he would have to pay me what those jobs were worth. Needless to say, that was unacceptable to him. I thought you wanted a part in the movie, he said. I never said that, I answered. Because if you do, he continued, we'll have to clear up this business first. Once again, I told him there was nothing to clear up. All right, he said, if that's how you feel about it, then we have nothing to say to each other anymore. And with that remark he turned away from me and told the driver to stop the car.

We had been riding around for about half an hour by then, slowly drifting toward the outer fringes of Paris, and the neighborhood where the car had stopped was unfamiliar to me. It was a cold January night, and I had no idea where I was, but the conversation was over, and there was nothing for me to do but say good-bye to him and get out of the car. If I remember correctly, we didn't even shake hands. I stepped out onto the sidewalk, shut the door, and the car drove off. And that was the end of my career in the movies.

I stayed on in France for another eighteen months—
half of them in Paris and half of them in Provence,
where my girlfriend and I worked as caretakers of a
farmhouse in the northern Var. By the time I returned
to New York, I had under ten dollars in my pocket
and not a single concrete plan for the future. I was
twenty-seven years old, and with nothing to show for
myself but a book of poems and a handful of obscure
literary essays, I was no closer to having solved the
problem of money than I'd been before I left America.
To further complicate the situation, my girlfriend and
I decided to get married. It was an impulsive move,
but with so many things about to change, we figured
why not go ahead and change everything at once?

I immediately began casting about for work. I
made telephone calls, followed up on leads, went in
for interviews, explored as many possibilities as I
could. I was trying to act sensibly, and after all the
ups and downs I'd been through, all the tight corners
and desperate squeezes that had trapped me over the
years, I was determined not to repeat my old mistakes.
I had learned my lesson, I told myself, and this time
I was going to take care of business.

But I hadn't, and I didn't. For all my high-minded
intentions, it turned out that I was incorrigible. It's
not that I didn't find a job, but rather than accept the
full-time position I had been offered (as junior editor

in a large publishing house), I opted for a half-time job at half the pay. I had vowed to swallow my medicine, but just when the spoon was coming toward me, I shut my mouth. Until it happened, I had no idea that I was going to balk like that, no idea how stubbornly I was going to resist. Against all the odds, it seemed that I still hadn't given up the vain and stupid hope of surviving on my own terms. A part-time job looked like a good solution, but not even that was enough. I wanted total independence, and when some freelance translation work finally came my way, I quit the job and went off on my own again. From start to finish, the experiment lasted just seven months. Short as that time might have been, it was the only period of my adult life when I earned a regular paycheck.

By every standard, the job I had found was an excellent one. My boss was Arthur Cohen, a man of many interests, much money, and a first-rate mind. A writer of both novels and essays, a former publishing executive, and a passionate collector of art, he had recently set up a little business as an outlet for his excess energies. Part hobbyhorse, part serious commercial venture, Ex Libris was a rare-book concern that specialized in publications connected with twentieth-century art. Not books *about* art, but manifestations of the art itself. Magazines from the Dada movement, for example, or books designed by mem-

bers of the Bauhaus, or photographs by Stieglitz, or
an edition of Ovid's *Metamorphoses* illustrated by Pi-
casso. As the back cover of each Ex Libris catalogue
announced: "Books and Periodicals in Original Editions for the Documentation of the Art of the 20th
Century: Futurism, Cubism, Dada, Bauhaus and
Constructivism, De Stijl, Surrealism, Expressionism,
Post War Art, as well as Architecture, Typography,
Photography and Design."

Arthur was just getting the operation off the
ground when he hired me as his sole employee. My
chief task was to help him write the Ex Libris catalogues, which were issued twice a year and ran to a
little over a hundred pages. Other duties included
writing letters, preparing the catalogues for bulk mail-
ings, fulfilling orders, and making tuna fish sand-
wiches for lunch. Mornings I spent at home, working
for myself, and at twelve o'clock I would go downstairs
to Riverside Drive and take the number 4 bus to the
office. An apartment had been rented in a brownstone
building on East Sixty-ninth Street to store Ex Libris's
holdings, and the two rooms were crammed with
thousands of books, magazines, and prints. Stacked
on tables, wedged onto shelves, piled high in closets,
these precious objects had overwhelmed the entire
space. I spent four or five hours there every afternoon,

and it was a bit like working in a museum, a small shrine to the avant-garde.

Arthur worked in one room and I worked in the other, each of us planted at a desk as we combed through the items for sale and prepared our meticulous catalogue entries on five-by-seven index cards. Anything having to do with French and English was given to me; Arthur handled the German and Russian materials. Typography, design, and architecture were his domain; I was in charge of all things literary. There was a certain fusty precision to the work (measuring the books, examining them for imperfections, detailing provenances when necessary), but many of the items were quite thrilling to hold, and Arthur gave me free rein to express my opinions about them, even to inject an occasional dose of humor if I felt like it. A few examples from the second catalogue will give some idea of what the job entailed:

233. DUCHAMP, M. & HALBERSTADT, V.
L'Opposition et les cases conjuguées sont réconciliées par M. Duchamp et V. Halberstadt. Editions de L'Echiquier. St. Germain-en-Laye and Brussels, 1932. Parallel text in German and English on left-hand pages. 112 double-numbered pp.,

with 2-color illustrations. 9 ⅝ × 11".
Printed paper covers.

The famous book on chess written and designed by Duchamp. (Schwarz, p. 589). Although it is a serious text, devoted to a real
chess problem, it is nevertheless so obscure
as to be virtually worthless. Schwarz quotes
Duchamp as having said: "The endgames
on which this fact turns are of no interest
to any chess player; and that's the funniest
thing about it. Only three or four people in
the world are interested in it, and they're
the ones who've tried the same lines of research as Halberstadt and myself, since we
wrote the book together. Chess champions
never read this book, because the problem
it poses never really turns up more than
once in a lifetime. These are possible end-
game problems, but they're so rare that
they're almost utopian." (p. 63). $1000.00

394. (STEIN, GERTRUDE). Testimony: Against
Gertrude Stein. Texts by Georges Braque,
Eugene Jolas, Maria Jolas, Henri Matisse,
André Salmon, Tristan Tzara. Servire Press.
The Hague, February, 1935. (Transition

Pamphlet no. 1; supplement to Transition 1934–1935; no. 23). 16 pp. 5¹¹⁄₁₆ × 8⅞". Printed paper covers. Stapled.

In light of the great Stein revival of the Seventies, the continuing value of this pamphlet cannot be denied. It serves as an antidote to literary self-serving and, in its own right, is an important document of literary and artistic history. Occasioned by the inaccuracies and distortions of fact in The Autobiography of Alice B. Toklas, Transition produced this forum in order to allow some of the figures treated in Miss Stein's book to rebut her portrayal of them. The verdict seems to be unanimous. Matisse: "In short, it is more like a harlequin's costume the different pieces of which, having been more or less invented by herself, have been sewn together without taste and without relation to reality." Eugene Jolas: "The Autobiography of Alice B. Toklas, in its hollow, tinsel bohemianism and egocentric deformations, may very well become one day the symbol of the decadence that hovers over contemporary literature." Braque: "Miss Stein understood nothing of what went on around her." Tzara: "Underneath the 'baby' style, which is pleasant enough when it is a question of simpering at the interstices of envy, it is easy to discern such a really coarse spirit, accustomed to the artifices of the lowest literary prostitution, that I cannot believe it necessary for me to insist on the presence of a clinical case of megalomania." Salmon: "And what confusion! What incomprehension of an epoch! Fortunately there are others who have described it better." Finally, the piece by Maria Jolas is particularly noteworthy for its detailed description of the early days of Transition. This pamphlet was originally not for sale separately. $95.00

437. GAUGUIN, PAUL. Noa Noa. Voyage de Tahiti. Les Editions G. Crès & Cie. Paris, 1924. 154 pp., illustrated with 22 woodcuts after Paul Gauguin by Daniel de Monfreid. 5¾ × 7¹⁵⁄₁₆". Illustrated paper wrappers over paper.

This is the first definitive edition, including introductory material and poems by

Charles Morice. The record of Gauguin's first two years in Tahiti, remarkable not only for its significant biographical revelations, but for its insightful anthropological approach to a strange culture. Gauguin follows Baudelaire's persuasive dictum: "Dites, qu'avez-vous vu?" and the result is this miracle of vision: a Frenchman, at the height of European colonialism, travelling to an "underdeveloped country" neither to conquer nor convert, but to learn. This experience is the central event of Gauguin's life, both as an artist and as a man. Also: Noa Noa, translated into English by O.F. Theis. Nicholas L. Brown. New York, 1920. (Fifth printing; first printing in 1919). 148 pp. + 10 Gauguin reproductions. $5\frac{5}{16}$ × $7\frac{13}{16}$". Paper and cloth over boards. (Some minor foxing in French edition; slight fraying of spine in both French and English editions.) $65.00

509. RAY, MAN. Mr. and Mrs. Woodman. Edition Unida. No place, 1970. Pages unnumbered; with 27 original photographs and 1 signed and numbered engraving by Man

Ray. 10½ × 11⅞". Leather bound, gilt-
edged cardboard pages; leather and mar-
bleized fitted box.

One of the very strangest of Man Ray's
many strange works. Mr. and Mrs. Woodman are two puppet-like wood figures con-
structed by Man Ray in Hollywood in 1947,
and the book, composed in 1970, is a series
of mounted photographs of these witty,
amazingly life-like characters in some of
the most contorted erotic postures imaginable. In some sense, this book can best
be described as a wood-people's guide to
sex. Of an edition of only 50 copies, this is
number 31, signed by Man Ray. All photographs are originals of the artist and carry
his mark. Inserted is an original, numbered
and signed engraving, specially made by
Man Ray for this edition. $2100.00

Arthur and I got along well, with no strain or conflict, and we worked together in a friendly, unruffled
atmosphere. Had I been a somewhat different person,
I might have held on to that job for years, but seeing
that I wasn't, I began to grow bored and restless after
a few months. I enjoyed looking through the material

I had to write about, but I didn't have the mind of a collector, and I could never bring myself to feel the proper awe or reverence for the things we sold. When you sit down to write about the catalogue that Marcel Duchamp designed for the 1947 Surrealist exhibition in Paris, for example—the one with the rubber breast on the cover, the celebrated bare falsie that came with the admonition *"Prière de Toucher"* ("Please Touch")— and you find that catalogue protected by several layers of bubble wrap, which in turn have been swathed in thick brown paper, which in turn has been slipped into a plastic bag, you can't help but pause for a moment and wonder if you aren't wasting your time. *Prière de toucher*. Duchamp's imperative is an obvious play on the signs you see posted all over France: *Prière de ne pas toucher* (Do Not Touch). He turns the warning on its head and asks us to fondle the thing he has made. And what better thing than this spongy, perfectly formed breast? Don't venerate it, he says, don't take it seriously, don't worship this frivolous activity we call art. Twenty-seven years later, the warning is turned upside down again. The naked breast has been covered. The thing to be touched has been made untouchable. The joke has been turned into a deadly serious transaction, and once again money has the last word.

This is not to criticize Arthur. No one loved these

things more than he did, and if the catalogues we mailed out to potential customers were vehicles of commerce, they were also works of scholarship, rigorous documents in their own right. The difference between us was not that I understood the issues any better than he did (if anything, it was just the opposite), but that he was a businessman and I wasn't, which explained why he was the boss and I made just a few measly dollars per hour. Arthur took pleasure in turning a profit, enjoyed the push and pull of running the enterprise and making it succeed, and while he was also a man of great sophistication and refinement, a genuine intellectual who lived in and for the world of ideas, there was no getting around the fact that he was a crafty entrepreneur. Apparently, a life of the mind was not incompatible with the pursuit of money. I understood myself well enough to know that such a thing wasn't possible for me, but I saw now that it was possible for others. Some people didn't have to choose. They didn't have to divide the world into two separate camps. They could actually live in both places at the same time.

A few weeks after I started working for him, Arthur recommended me to a friend who was looking to hire someone for a short-term job. Arthur knew that I could use the extra money, and I mention this small favor as an example of how well he treated me. That

the friend turned out to be Jerzy Kosinski, and that
the job involved me in editing the manuscript of Kosinski's latest book, makes the episode worth talking
about a little more. Intense controversy has surrounded Kosinski in recent years, and since a large
share of it emanated from the novel I worked on
(*Cockpit*), I feel that I should add my testimony to the
record. As Arthur explained it to me, the job was a
simple matter of looking through the manuscript and
making sure that the English was in good order. Since
English wasn't Kosinski's first language, it seemed
perfectly reasonable to me that he should want to have
the prose checked before he handed the book to his
publisher. What I didn't know was that other people
had worked on the manuscript before me—three or
four others, depending on which account you read.
Kosinski never mentioned this earlier help to me, but
whatever problems the book still had were not because the English didn't sound like English. The flaws
were more fundamental than that, more about the
book itself than how the story was told. I corrected a
few sentences here, changed a few words there, but
the novel was essentially finished by the time the
manuscript was given to me. If left to my own devices,
I could have completed the work in one or two days,
but because Kosinski wouldn't let the manuscript out
of his house, I had to go to his apartment on West

Fifty-seventh Street to do the work, and because he hovered around me constantly, interrupting me every twenty minutes with stories, anecdotes, and nervous chatter, the job dragged on for seven days. I don't know why, but Kosinski seemed terribly eager to impress me, and the truth was that he did. He was so thoroughly high-strung, so odd and manic in his behavior, that I couldn't help but be impressed. What made these interruptions doubly odd and intriguing was that nearly every story he told me also appeared in the book he had written—the very novel spread out before me when he came into the room to talk. How he had masterminded his escape from Poland, for example. Or how he would prowl around Times Square at two in the morning disguised as a Puerto Rican undercover cop. Or how, occasionally, he would turn up at expensive restaurants dressed in a sham military uniform (made for him by his tailor and representing no identifiable rank, country, or branch of service), but because that uniform looked good, and because it was covered with countless medals and stars, he would be given the best table in the house by the awestruck maître d'—without a reservation, without a tip, without so much as a glance. The book was supposedly a work of fiction, but when Kosinski told me these stories, he presented them as facts, real events from his life. Did he know the difference? I can't be sure, can't even begin to guess, but if I had to give an answer, I would say that he did. He struck me as too clever, too cunningly aware of himself and his effect on others not to enjoy the confusion he created. The common theme in the stories was deception, after all, playing people for fools, and from the way he laughed when he told them—as if gloating, as if reveling in his own cynicism—I felt that perhaps he was only toying with me, buttering me up with compliments in order to test the limits of my credulity. Perhaps. And then again, perhaps not. The only thing I know for certain is that Kosinski was a man of labyrinthine complexity. When the rumors started circulating about him in the mid-eighties and magazine articles began to appear with accusations of plagiarism and the use of ghost writers and false claims concerning his past, I wasn't surprised. Years later, when he took his own life by suffocating himself with a plastic bag, I was. He died in the same apartment where I had worked for him in 1974, in the same bathroom where I had washed my hands and used the toilet. I have only to think about it for a moment, and I can see it all.

Otherwise, my months at Ex Libris passed quietly. Nothing much happened, and since most of the business was conducted through the mail, it was a rare day when anyone came to the apartment and disturbed us at our work. Late one afternoon, however, when Arthur was out on an errand, John Lennon knocked on the door, wanting to look at Man Ray photographs.

"Hi," he said, thrusting out his hand at me, "I'm John."

"Hi," I said, taking hold of the hand and giving it a good shake, "I'm Paul."

As I searched for the photographs in one of the closets, Lennon stopped in front of the Robert Motherwell canvas that hung on the wall beside Arthur's desk. There wasn't much to the painting—a pair of straight black lines against a broad orange background—and after studying it for a few moments, he turned to me and said, "Looks like that one took a lot of work, huh?" With all the pieties floating around the art world, I found it refreshing to hear him say that.

Arthur and I parted on good terms, with no hard feelings on either side. I made it my business to find a replacement for myself before I quit, and that made my departure relatively simple and painless. We stayed in touch for a little while, occasionally calling each other to catch up on the news, but eventually we lost contact, and when Arthur died of leukemia several years ago, I couldn't even remember the last time I had talked to him. Then came Kosinski's suicide. Add that to John Lennon's murder more than a decade earlier, and nearly everyone associated with the

months I spent in that office has disappeared. Even
Arthur's friend Robert Motherwell, the good artist responsible for the bad painting that provoked Lennon's
comment, is no longer with us. Reach a certain moment in your life, and you discover that your days are
spent as much with the dead as they are with the
living.

The next two years were an intensely busy time. Between March 1975, when I stopped working for Ex
Libris, and June 1977, when my son was born, I came
out with two more books of poetry, wrote several one-
act plays, published fifteen or twenty critical pieces,
and translated half a dozen books with my wife, Lydia
Davis. These translations were our primary source of
income, and we worked together as a team, earning
so many dollars per thousand words and taking whatever jobs we were offered. Except for one book by
Sartre (*Life/Situations*, a collection of essays and interviews), the books the publishers gave us were dull,
undistinguished works that ranged in quality from not
very good to downright bad. The money was bad as
well, and even though our rate kept increasing from
book to book, if you broke down what we did on an
hourly basis, we were scarcely a penny or two ahead
of the minimum wage. The key was to work fast, to

crank out the translations as quickly as we could and never stop for breath. There are surely more inspiring ways to make a living, but Lydia and I tackled these jobs with great discipline. A publisher would hand us a book, we would split the work in two (literally tearing the book in half if we had only one copy), and set a daily quota for ourselves. Nothing was allowed to interfere with that number. So many pages had to be done every day, and every day, whether we felt in the mood or not, we sat down and did them. Flipping hamburgers would have been just as lucrative, but at least we were free, or at least we thought we were free, and I never felt any regrets about having left my job. For better or worse, this was how I had chosen to live. Between translating for money and writing for myself, there was rarely a moment during those years when I wasn't sitting at my desk, putting words on a piece of paper.

I didn't write criticism for money, but I was paid for most of the articles I published, and that helped pad my income to a certain degree. Still, getting by was a struggle, and from month to month we were no more than a short dry spell away from real poverty. Then, in the fall of 1975, just half a year into this tightrope walk *à deux*, my luck turned. I was given a five-thousand-dollar grant from the Ingram Merrill Foundation, and for the next little while the worst of the pressure was off. The money was so unexpected, so enormous in its ramifications, that I felt as if an angel had dropped down from the sky and kissed me on the forehead.

The man most responsible for this stroke of good fortune was John Bernard Myers. John didn't give me the money out of his own pocket, but he was the person who told me about the foundation and encouraged me to apply for the grant. The real benefactor, of course, was the poet James Merrill. In the quietest, most discreet manner possible, he had been sharing his family's wealth with other writers and artists for many years, hiding behind his middle name so as not to call attention to his astounding generosity. A committee met every six months to consider new applications and to dole out the awards. John was secretary of the committee, and although he didn't take part in choosing the recipients, he sat in on the meetings and knew how the members thought. Nothing was sure, he said, but he suspected that they would be inclined to support my work. So I put together a sampling of my poems and sent them in. At the next semiannual meeting, John's hunch proved to be correct.

I don't think I've ever known a funnier or more effusive person than John. When I first met him, in late 1974, he had been an integral part of the New York scene for the past thirty years, most famously as director of the Tibor de Nagy Gallery in the fifties, but also as cofounder of the Artists Theatre, editor of various short-lived literary magazines, and all-around champion and impresario of young talent. John was the first to give major shows to such artists as Red Grooms, Larry Rivers, Helen Frankenthaler, and Fairfield Porter, and he published the first books of Frank O'Hara, John Ashbery, and other poets of the New York School. The plays he produced were collaborations between many of these same poets and painters—O'Hara and Rivers, for example, or James Schuyler and Elaine de Kooning, the one writing the words and the other designing the sets. The Artists Theatre didn't bring in much at the box office, but John and his partner kept it running for years, and at a time when Off Broadway had yet to come into being, it was about the only experimental theater available in New York. What set John apart from all the other dealers, publishers, and producers I've known is that he wasn't in it for the money. Truth be told, he probably wasn't much of a businessman, but he had a genuine passion for art in all its forms, rigorous standards, openness of spirit, and an immense hunger for work that was different, challenging, new. A large man of six-three or six-four, he often made me think of John Wayne in his physical appearance. This John, however, in that he was proudly and flagrantly homosexual, in that he gleefully mocked himself with all manner of mincing gestures and extravagant poses, in that he took delight in silly jokes and ridiculous songs and a whole repertoire of childish humor, had nothing to do with that other John. No tough guy stuff for him. This John was all enthusiasm and goodwill, a man who had dedicated his life to beautiful things, and he wore his heart on his sleeve.*

When I met him, he was just starting up a new magazine—"of words and pictures"—called *Parenthèse*. I can't remember who suggested that I send him my work, but I did, and from then on John made a point of putting something of mine in nearly every issue. Later, when he discontinued the magazine and began publishing books instead, the first title on the list was a collection of my poems. John's belief in my work was absolute, and he backed me at a time when few people even knew that I was alive. In the endnotes to *Parenthèse* 4, for example, buried among the dry accounts of contributors' past achievements, he took it upon himself to declare that "Paul Auster has created a stir in the literary world by his brilliant analysis of the work of Laura Riding Jackson, by his essays on French paintings, and his poetry." It didn't

---

*For a vivid account of his adventures, see John's *Tracking the Marvelous: A Life in the New York Art World*, published by Random House in 1983.

matter that this statement wasn't true, that John was
the only one paying attention. *Someone* was behind
me, and in those early days of struggle and uncer-
tainty, of not stirring up much of anything, that en-
couragement made all the difference. John was the
first person who took a stand for me, and I have never
stopped feeling grateful to him for that.

When the grant money came, Lydia and I hit the
road again. We sublet our apartment and went to
the Laurentian Mountains in Quebec, holing up in the
house of a painter friend for a couple of months while
he was away, then returned to New York for a week
or two, and then promptly packed our bags again and
took a cross-country train to San Francisco. We eventually settled in Berkeley, renting a small efficiency
apartment not far from the university, and lived there
for six months. We weren't flush enough to stop translating, but the pace was less frantic now, and that
allowed me to spend more time with my own work. I
went on writing poems, but new impulses and ideas
started coming as well, and before long I found myself
writing a play. That led to another play, which in turn
led to another play, and when I returned to New York
in the fall, I showed them to John. I didn't know what
to make of what I had written. The pieces had surged
up unexpectedly, and the results were quite different
from anything I had done before. When John told me

he liked them, I felt that perhaps I had taken a step in the right direction. The farthest thing from my mind was to do anything with them in a practical sense. I had given no thought to having them performed, no thought to publishing them. As far as I was concerned, they were hardly more than spare, minimalist exercises, an initial stab at something that might or might not turn out to be real. When John said that he wanted to take the longest of the plays and mount a production of it, I was caught totally by surprise.

No one was to blame for what happened. John jumped in with his customary excitement and energy, but things kept going wrong, and after a while it began to seem that we weren't putting on a play so much as trying to prove the indestructible power of Murphy's Law. A director and three actors were found, and shortly after that a reading was scheduled to drum up financial support for the production. That was the plan, in any case. It didn't help that the actors were young and inexperienced, not up to the task of delivering their lines with conviction or true feeling, but even worse was the audience who came to hear them deliver those lines. John had invited a dozen of his richest art collector friends, and not one of these potential backers was under sixty or had the slightest interest in the theater. He was counting on the play to seduce them, to overwhelm their hearts and minds

with such stunning finality that they would feel no
choice but to reach into their pockets and start pulling
out their checkbooks. The event was held at a posh
Upper East Side apartment, and my job was to charm
these wealthy patrons, to smile and chat and reassure
them that they were putting their money on the right
horse. The problem was that I had no talent for smiling and chatting. I arrived in a state of extreme tension, nervous to the point of being ill, and quickly
downed two bourbons to undo the knot in my stomach.
The alcohol had precisely the opposite effect, and by
the time the reading started, I had come down with a
massive headache, a blistering, brain-bending assault
that grew ever more unbearable as the evening wore
on. The play thudded forward, and from start to finish
the rich people sat in silence, utterly unmoved. Lines
that I had imagined were funny did not produce the
faintest titter. They were bored by the gags, indifferent
to the pathos, perplexed by the whole thing. At the
end, after some grim, perfunctory applause, I could
only think about how to get out of there and hide. My
head was cracking with pain. I felt stabbed and hu-
miliated, unable to speak, but I couldn't abandon
John, and so for the next half hour I listened to him
talk about the play to his befuddled friends, doing
everything I could not to pass out on the carpet. John
put up a brave front, but every time he turned to me

for help, I could do no more than stare down at my shoes and mumble a brief, unintelligible comment. Finally, apropos of nothing, I blurted out some lame excuse and left.

A lesser man would have given up after such a defeat, but John was undaunted. Not a penny of aid emerged from that gruesome evening, but he went ahead and started improvising a new plan, scuttling his dream of theatrical glory for a more modest, workable approach. If we couldn't afford a real theater, he said, we would make do with something else. The play was the only thing that mattered, and even if the run was limited to just a single, invitation-only performance, there was going to be a production of my play. If not for me, he said, and if not for him, then at least for his friend Herbert Machiz, who had died that summer. Herbert had directed the plays at the old Artists Theatre, and because he had been John's companion for twenty-five years, John was determined to revive the Theatre in Herbert's memory—if only for just one night.

A man who owned a restoration studio on East Sixty-ninth Street offered John the use of his space. It happened to be just down the block from the Ex Libris office—an interesting, if minor, coincidence— but more to the point was that in its previous incarnation the carriage house where John's friend now worked had been the studio of Mark Rothko. Rothko had killed himself there in 1970, and now, less than seven years later, my play was going to be presented in that same room. I don't want to sound overly superstitious about it, but given how things turned out, it feels that we were cursed, that no matter what any of us did or didn't do, the project was bound to fail.

Preparations began. The director and the three actors worked hard, and little by little the performances improved. I wouldn't go so far as to call them good, but at least they were no longer an embarrassment. One of the actors stood out from the others, and as the rehearsals went on, I began to pin my hopes on him, praying that his inventiveness and daring might pull the production up to a reasonably competent level. A date in early March was chosen for the performance, invitations were sent out, and arrangements were made for a hundred and fifty folding chairs to be delivered to the carriage house. I should have known better, but I actually began to feel optimistic. Then, just days before the big night, the good actor came down with pneumonia, and because there were no understudies (how could there have been?), it looked as if the performance would have to be canceled. The actor, however, who had put weeks of time and effort into the rehearsals, was not about to give up. In spite of a high temperature, in spite of the fact that he was coughing up blood just hours before the play was supposed to start, he crawled out of bed, pumped his system full of antibiotics, and staggered on at the appointed time. It was the noblest of noble gestures, the gutsy act of a born trouper, and I was impressed by his courage—no, more than impressed: filled with admiration—but the sad truth was that he was in no shape to do what he did. Everything that had sparkled in the rehearsals suddenly lost its shine. The performance was flat, the timing was off, scene after scene was blown. I stood at the back of the room and watched, powerless to do a thing. I saw my little play die in front of a hundred and fifty people, and I couldn't lift a finger to stop it.

Before putting the whole miserable experience behind me, I sat down and reworked the play. The performances had been only part of the problem, and I wasn't about to palm off responsibility for what had happened on the director or the actors. The play was too long, I realized, too rambling and diffuse, and radical surgery was needed to mend it. I began chopping and trimming, hacking away at everything that felt weak or superfluous, and by the time I was finished, half of the play was gone, one of the characters had been eliminated, and the title had been changed. I typed up this new version, now called *Laurel and Hardy Go to Heaven*, put it in a folder along with the other two plays I had written (*Blackouts* and *Hide and Seek*), and stuck the folder in a drawer of my desk. My plan was to keep it there and never look inside the drawer again.

Three months after the flop of the play, my son was born. Watching Daniel come into the world was a moment of supreme happiness for me, an event of such magnitude that even as I broke down and wept at the sight of his small body and held him in my arms for the first time, I understood that the world had changed, that I had passed from one state of being into another. Fatherhood was the dividing line, the great wall that stood between youth and adulthood, and I was on the other side now forever.

I was glad to be there. Emotionally, spiritually, and even physically, there was nowhere else I wanted to be, and I was fully prepared to take on the demands of living in this new place. Financially, however, I wasn't the least bit prepared for anything. You pay a toll when you climb over that wall, and by the time I landed on the other side, my pockets were nearly empty. Lydia and I had left New York by then, moving to a house about two hours up the Hudson, and it was there that the hard times finally hit. The storm lasted for eighteen months, and when the wind died down enough for me to crawl out of my hole and inspect the damage, I saw that everything was gone. The entire landscape had been leveled.

Moving out of the city was the first step in a long series of miscalculations. We figured we could live on less money in the country, but the plain fact was that we couldn't. Car expenses, heating expenses, house repairs, and pediatrician's bills ate up whatever advantage we thought we had gained, and before long we were working so hard just to make ends meet that there was no time left for anything else. In the past, I had always managed to keep a few hours to myself every day, to push on with my poems and writing projects after spending the first part of the day working for money. Now, as our need for money rose, there was less time available to me for my own work. I started missing a day, then two days, then a week, and after a while I lost my rhythm as a writer. When I did manage to find some time for myself, I was too tense to write very well. Months went by, and every piece of paper I touched with my pen wound up in the garbage.

By the end of 1977, I was feeling trapped, desperate to find a solution. I had spent my whole life avoiding the subject of money, and now, suddenly, I could think of nothing else. I dreamed of miraculous reversals, lottery millions falling down from the sky, outrageous get-rich-quick schemes. Even the ads on matchbook covers began to hold a certain fascination. "Make Money Growing Worms in Your Basement." Now that I lived in a house with a basement, don't think I wasn't tempted. My old way of doing things had led to disaster, and I was ripe for new ideas, a new way of tackling the dilemma that had dogged me from the start: how to reconcile the needs of the body with the needs of the soul. The terms of the equation were still the same: time on the one hand, money on the other. I had gambled on being able to manage both, but after years of trying to feed first one mouth, then two mouths, and then three mouths, I had finally lost. It wasn't difficult to understand why. I had put too much of myself into working for time and not enough into working for money, and the result was that now I didn't have either one.

In early December, a friend came up from the city to visit for a few days. We had known each other since college, and he, too, had turned into a struggling writer—yet one more Columbia graduate without a pot to piss in. If anything, he was having an even rougher time of it than I was. Most of his work was unpublished, and he supported himself by bouncing from one pathetic temporary job to another, aimlessly traveling around the country in search of strange, down-and-out adventures. He had recently landed in New York again and was working in a toy store somewhere in Manhattan, part of the brigade of surplus help who stand behind the counters during the Christmas shopping season. I picked him up at the train station, and during the half-hour ride back to the house, we talked mostly about toys and games, the things he sold in the store. For reasons that still mystify me, this conversation dislodged a small pebble that had been stuck somewhere in my unconscious, an obstruction that had been sitting over a tiny pinprick hole of memory, and now that I was able to look down that hole again, I found something that had been lost for nearly twenty years. Back when I was ten or twelve, I had invented a game. Using an ordinary deck of fifty-two playing cards, I had sat down on my bed one afternoon and figured out a way to play baseball with them. Now, as I went on talking to my friend in the car, the game came rushing back to me. I remembered everything about it: the basic principles, the rules, the whole setup down to the last detail.

Under normal circumstances, I probably would have forgotten all about it again. But I was a desperate man, a man with my back against the wall, and I knew that if I didn't think of something fast, the firing squad was about to fill my body with bullets. A windfall was the only way out of my predicament. If I could rustle up a nice large chunk of cash, the nightmare would suddenly stop. I could bribe off the soldiers, walk out of the prison yard, and go home to become a writer again. If translating books and writing magazine articles could no longer do the job, then I owed it to myself and my family to try something else. Well, people bought games, didn't they? What if I worked up my old baseball game into something good, something really good, and managed to sell it? Maybe I'd get lucky and find my bag of gold, after all.

It almost sounds like a joke now, but I was in dead earnest. I knew that my chances were next to nil, but once the idea grabbed hold of me, I couldn't shake free of it. Nuttier things had happened, I told myself, and if I wasn't willing to put a little time and effort into having a go at it, then what kind of spineless shit was I?

The game from my childhood had been organized around a few simple operations. The pitcher turned over cards: each red card from ace to 10 was a strike; each black card from ace to 10 was a ball. If a face card was turned over, that meant the batter swung. The batter then turned over a card. Anything from ace to 9 was an out, with each out corresponding to the position numbers of the defensive players: Pitcher=ace (1); Catcher=2; First Baseman=3; Second Baseman=4; third baseman=5; Shortstop=6; Left Fielder=7; Center Fielder=8; Right Fielder=9.

If the batter turned over a 5, for example, that meant the out was made by the third baseman. A black 5 indicated a ground ball; a red 5 indicated a ball hit in the air (diamond=pop-up; heart=line drive). On balls hit to the outfield (7, 8, 9), black indicated a shallow fly ball, red a deep fly ball. Turn over a 10, and you had yourself a single. A jack was a double, a queen was a triple, and a king was a home run.

It was crude but reasonably effective, and while the distribution of hits was mathematically off (there should have been more singles than doubles, more doubles than home runs, and more home runs than triples), the games were often close and exciting. More important, the final scores looked like the scores of real baseball games—3 to 2, 7 to 4, 8 to 0—and not football or basketball games. The fundamental principles were sound. All I had to do was get rid of the standard deck and design a new set of cards. That would allow me to make the game statistically accurate, add new elements of strategy and decision making (bunts, stolen bases, sacrifice flies), and lift the whole thing to a higher level of subtlety and sophistication. The work was largely a matter of getting the numbers right and fiddling with the math, but I was well versed in the intricacies of baseball, and it didn't take me long to arrive at the correct formulas. I played out game after game after game, and at the end of a

couple of weeks there were no more adjustments to
be made. Then came the tedious part. Once I had
designed the cards (two decks of ninety-six cards
each), I had to sit down with four fine-tipped pens
(one red, one green, one black, one blue) and draw
the cards by hand. I can't remember how many days
it took me to complete this task, but by the time I
came to the end, I felt as if I had never done anything
else. The design was nothing to brag about, but since
I had no experience or talent as a designer, that was
to be expected. I was striving for a clear, serviceable
presentation, something that could be read at a glance
and not confuse anyone, and given that so much information had to be crammed onto every card, I think
I accomplished at least that. Beauty and elegance
could come later. If anyone showed enough interest to
want to manufacture the game, the problem could be
turned over to a professional designer. For the time
being, after much dithering back and forth, I dubbed
my little brainchild Action Baseball.

Once again, my stepfather came to the rescue. He
happened to have a friend who worked for one of the
largest, most successful American toy companies, and
when I showed the game to this man, he was impressed by it, thought it had a real chance of appealing to someone. I was still working on the cards at
that point, but he encouraged me to get the game in

order as quickly as I could and take it to the New York Toy Fair, which was just five or six weeks down the road. I had never heard of it, but by all accounts it was the most important annual event in the business. Every February, companies from around the world gathered at the Toy Center at Twenty-third Street and Fifth Avenue to display their products for the upcoming season, take note of what the competition was up to, and make plans for the future. What the Frankfurt Book Fair is for books and the Cannes Film Festival is for films, the New York Toy Fair is for toys. My stepfather's friend took charge of everything for me. He arranged to have my name put on the list of "inventors," which qualified me for a badge and an open pass to the fair, and then, as if that weren't enough, set up an appointment for me to meet with the president of his company—at nine o'clock in the morning on the first day of the fair.

I was grateful for the help, but at the same time I felt like someone who had just been booked on a flight to an unknown planet. I had no idea what to expect, no map of the terrain, no guidebook to help me understand the habits and customs of the creatures I would be talking to. The only solution I could think of was to wear a jacket and tie. The tie was the only one I owned, and it hung in my closet for emergency use at weddings and funerals. Now business meetings could be added to the list. I must have cut a ridiculous figure as I strode into the Toy Center that morning to collect my badge. I was carrying a briefcase, but the only thing inside it was the game, which was stowed inside a cigar box. That was all I had: the game itself, along with several Xeroxed copies of the rules. I was about to go in and talk to the president of a multimillion-dollar business, and I didn't even have a business card.

Even at that early hour, the place was swarming with people. Everywhere you turned, there were endless rows of corporate stands, display booths decked out with dolls and puppets and fire engines and dinosaurs and extraterrestrials. Every kiddie amusement and gadget ever dreamed of was packed into that hall, and there wasn't one of them that didn't whistle or clang or toot or beep or roar. As I made my way through the din, it occurred to me that the briefcase under my arm was the only silent object in the building. Computer games were all the rage that year, the biggest thing to hit the toy world since the invention of the wind-up jack-in-the-box, and I was hoping to strike it rich with an old-fashioned deck of cards. Maybe I would, but until I walked into that noisy fun house, I hadn't realized how likely it was that I wouldn't.

My talk with the company president turned out to

be one of the shortest meetings in the annals of American business. It didn't bother me that the man rejected my game (I was prepared for that, was fully expecting bad news), but he did it in such a chilling way, with so little regard for human decency, that it still causes me pain to think about it. He wasn't much older than I was, this corporate executive, and with his sleek, superbly tailored suit, his blue eyes and blond hair and hard, expressionless face, he looked and acted like the leader of a Nazi spy ring. He barely shook my hand, barely said hello, barely acknowledged that I was in the room. No small talk, no pleasantries, no questions. "Let's see what you have," he said curtly, and so I reached into my briefcase and pulled out the cigar box. Contempt flickered in his eyes. It was as if I had just handed him a dog turd and asked him to smell it. I opened the box and took out the cards. By then, I could see that all hope was gone, that he had already lost interest, but there was nothing to do but forge ahead and start playing the game. I shuffled the decks, said something about how to read the three levels of information on the cards, and then got down to it. One or two batters into the top half of the first inning, he stood up from his chair and extended his hand to me. Since he hadn't spoken a word, I had no idea why he wanted to shake my hand. I continued to turn over cards, describing the action as it unfolded: ball, strike, swing. "Thank you," the Nazi said, finally taking hold of my hand. I still couldn't figure out what was going on. "Are you saying you don't want to see any more?" I said. "I haven't even had a chance to show you how it works." "Thank you," he said again. "You can leave now." Without another word, he turned and left me with my cards, which were still spread out on the table. It took me a minute or two to put everything back in the cigar box, and it was precisely then, during those sixty or ninety seconds, that I hit bottom, that I reached what I still consider to be the low point of my life.

Somehow or other, I managed to regroup. I went out for breakfast, pulled myself together, and returned to the fair for the rest of the day. One by one, I visited every game company I could find, shook hands, smiled, knocked on doors, demonstrated the wonders of Action Baseball to anyone willing to spare me ten or fifteen minutes. The results were uniformly discouraging. Most of the big companies had stopped working with independent inventors (too many lawsuits), and the small ones either wanted pocket-sized computer games (beep-beep) or else refused to look at anything connected with sports (low sales). At least these people were polite. After the sadistic treatment I'd been given that morning, I found some consolation in that.

Some time in the late afternoon, exhausted from hours of fruitless effort, I stumbled onto a company that specialized in card games. They had produced only one game so far, but that one had been wildly successful, and now they were in the market for a second. It was a small, low-budget operation run by two guys from Joliet, Illinois, a back-porch business with none of the corporate trappings and slick promotional methods of the other companies at the fair. That was a promising sign, but best of all, both partners admitted to being avid baseball fans. They weren't doing much at that hour, just sitting around their little booth and chewing the fat, and when I told them about my game, they seemed more than happy to have a look at it. Not just a peek, but a thorough viewing—to sit down and play a full nine-inning contest to the end.

If I had rigged the cards, the results of the game I played with them could not have been more exciting, more true to life. It was nip and tuck the whole way, tension riding on every pitch, and after eight and a half innings of threats, rallies, and two-out strikeouts with the bases loaded, the score stood at two to one. The Joliet boys were the home team, and when they came up for their last turn at bat, they needed a run to tie and two to win. The first two batters did nothing, and quickly they were down to their last out, with no runners on base. The following batter singled, however, to keep them alive. Then, to everyone's astonishment, with the count at two balls and two strikes, the next batter hit a home run to win the game. I couldn't have asked for more than that. A two-out, two-run homer in the bottom of the ninth inning to steal a victory on the last pitch. It was a classic baseball thriller, and when the man from Joliet turned over that final card, his face lit up with an expression of pure, undisguisable joy.

They wanted to think about it, they said, to mull it over for a while before giving me an answer. They would need a deck to study on their own, of course, and I told them I would send a color Xerox copy to Joliet as soon as possible. That was how we left it: shaking hands and exchanging addresses, promising each other to be in touch. After all the dismal, demoralizing events of that day, there was suddenly cause for hope, and I walked out of the Toy Fair thinking that I might actually get somewhere with my crazy scheme.

Color Xeroxing was a new process then, and it cost me a small fortune to have the copies made. I can't remember the exact amount, but it was more than a hundred dollars, I think, perhaps even two hundred. I shipped the package off to them and prayed they would write back soon. Weeks passed, and as I struggled to concentrate on the other work I had to do, it gradually dawned on me that I was in for a disappointment. Enthusiasm meant speed, indecision meant delay, and the longer they delayed, the worse the odds would be. It took almost two months for them to answer, and by then I didn't even have to read the letter to know what was in it. What surprised me was its brevity, its utter lack of personal warmth. I had spent close to an hour with them, had felt I'd entertained them and aroused their interest, but their rejection consisted of just one dry, clumsily written paragraph. Half the words were misspelled, and nearly every sentence had a grammatical error in it. It was an embarrassing document, a letter written by dunces, and once my hurt began to wear off a little, I felt ashamed of myself for having misjudged them so thoroughly. Put your faith in fools, and you end up fooling only yourself.

Still, I wasn't quite ready to give up. I had gone too far to allow one setback to throw me off course, and so I put my head down and plunged ahead. Until I had exhausted all the possibilities, I felt duty bound to continue, to see the whole misbegotten business through to the end. My in-laws put me in touch with a man who worked for Ruder and Finn, a prominent New York public relations firm. He loved the game, seemed genuinely enthused when I showed it to him,

and made an all-out effort to help. That was part of
the problem. Everyone liked Action Baseball, enough
people at any rate to keep me from abandoning it, and
with a kind, friendly, well-connected man like this one
pushing on my behalf, it wouldn't have made sense to
give up. My new ally's name was George, and he happened to be in charge of the General Foods account,
one of Ruder and Finn's most important clients. His
plan, which struck me as ingenious, was to get General Foods to put Action Baseball on the Wheaties
box as a special coupon offer. ("Hey, kids! Just mail
in two Wheaties box tops and a check or money order
for $3.98, and this incredible game can be yours!")
George proposed it to them, and for a time it looked
as if it might happen. Wheaties was considering ideas
for a new promotional campaign, and he thought this
one might just do the trick. It didn't. They went with
the Olympic decathlon champion instead, and for the
next umpteen years, every box of Wheaties was
adorned with a picture of Bruce Jenner's smiling face.
You can't really fault them. It was the Breakfast of
Champions, after all, and they had a certain tradition
to uphold. I never found out how close George came
to getting his idea through, but I must confess (somewhat reluctantly) that I still find it hard to look at a
box of Wheaties without feeling a little twinge.

George was almost as disappointed as I was, but now that he'd caught the bug, he wasn't about to quit trying. He knew someone in Indianapolis who was involved with the Babe Ruth League (in what capacity I forget) and thought something good might happen if he put me in contact with this man. The game was duly shipped to the Midwest again, and then followed another inordinately long silence. As the man hastened to explain to me when he finally wrote, he wasn't entirely responsible for the delay: "I am sorry to be so late in acknowledging receipt of your June 22 letter and your game, Action Baseball. They were late reaching me because of a tornado that wiped out our offices. I've been working at home since and did not get my mail until ten days or so ago." My bad luck was taking on an almost biblical dimension, and when the man wrote again several weeks later to tell me that he was passing on my game (sadly, with much regret, in the most courtly terms possible), I barely even flinched. "There is no question that your game is unique, innovative and interesting. There may well be a market for it since it is the only table-top base-ball game without a lot of trappings, which makes it faster-moving, but the consensus here is that without big league players and their statistics, the established competition is insurmountable." I called George to give him the news and thank him for his help, but enough was enough, I said, and he shouldn't waste any more time on me.

Things stalled for a couple of months after that, but then another lead materialized, and I picked up my lance and sallied forth again. As long as there was a windmill somewhere in sight, I was prepared to do battle with it. I had not the least shred of hope anymore, but I couldn't quite let go of the stupid thing I had started. My stepfather's younger brother knew a man who had invented a game, and since that game had earned him a pile of money, it seemed reasonable for me to contact him and ask for advice. We met in the lobby of the Roosevelt Hotel, not far from Grand Central Station. He was a fast-talking wheeler-dealer of around forty, a wholly antipathetical man with every kind of bluff and angle up his sleeve, but I must admit that his patter had some verve to it.

"Mail order," he said, "that's the ticket. Approach a major-league star, get him to endorse the game for a share of the profits, and then take out ads in all the baseball magazines. If enough orders come in, use the money to produce the game. If not, send the money back and call it quits."

"How much would a thing like that cost?" I asked.

"Twenty, twenty-five thousand dollars. Minimum."

"I couldn't come up with that much," I said. "Not even if my life depended on it."

"Then you can't do it, can you?"

"No, I can't do it. I just want to sell the game to a company. That's all I've ever had in mind—to make some royalties from the copies they sold. I wouldn't be capable of going into business for myself."

"In other words," the man said, finally realizing what a numskull he was talking to, "you've taken a shit, and now you want someone to flush the toilet for you."

That wasn't quite how I would have expressed it myself, but I didn't argue with him. He clearly knew more than I did, and when he went on to recommend that I find a "game broker" to talk to the companies for me, I didn't doubt that he was pointing me in the right direction. Until then, I hadn't even known of the existence of such people. He gave me the name of someone who was supposed to be particularly good, and I called her the next day. That turned out to be my last move, the final chapter of the whole muddled saga. She talked a mile a minute to me, outlining terms, conditions, and percentages, what to do and what not to do, what to expect and what to avoid. It sounded like her standard spiel, a furious condensation of years of hard knocks and cutthroat maneuvers, and for the first several minutes I couldn't get a word

in edgewise. Then, finally, she paused to catch her
breath, and that was when she asked me about my
game.

"It's called Action Baseball," I said.

"Did you say *baseball?*" she said.

"Yes, baseball. You turn over cards. It's very re-
alistic, and you can get through a full nine-inning
game in about fifteen minutes."

"Sorry," she said. "No sports games."

"What do you mean?"

"They're losers. They don't sell, and nobody wants
them. I wouldn't touch your game with a ten-foot
pole."

That did it for me. With the woman's blunt pro-
nouncement still ringing in my ears, I hung up the
phone, put the cards away, and stopped thinking about
them forever.

Little by little, I was coming to the end of my rope.
After the grim, garbled letter from Joliet, I understood
that Action Baseball was no more than a long shot.
To count on it as a source of money would have been
an act of pure self-deception, a ludicrous error. I
plugged away at it for several more months, but those
final efforts took up only a small fraction of my time.
Deep down, I had already accepted defeat—not just

of the game, not just of my half-assed foray into the business world, but of all my principles, my lifelong stand toward work, money, and the pursuit of time. Time didn't count anymore. I had needed it in order to write, but now that I was an ex-writer, a writer who wrote only for the satisfaction of crumpling up paper and throwing it in the garbage, I was ready to abandon the struggle and live like everyone else. Nine years of freelance penury had burned me out. I had tried to rescue myself by inventing the game, but no one had wanted the game, and now I was right back where I had been—only worse, only more burned out than ever. At least the game had represented an idea, a temporary surge of hope, but now I had run out of ideas as well. The truth was that I had dug myself into a deep, dark hole, and the only way to crawl out of it was to find a job.

I made calls, wrote letters, traveled down to the city for interviews. Teaching jobs, journalism jobs, editorial jobs—it didn't matter what it was. As long as the job came with a weekly paycheck, I was interested. Two or three things almost panned out, but in the end they didn't. I won't go into the depressing details now, but several months went by without any tangible results. I sank further into confusion, my mind almost paralyzed with worry. I had made a total surrender, had capitulated on every point I had defended over the years, and still I was getting nowhere, was losing ground with every step I took. Then, out of the blue, a grant of thirty-five hundred dollars came in from the New York State Council on the Arts, and I was given an unexpected breather. It wouldn't last long, but it was something—enough to ward off the hour of doom for another minute or two.

One night not long after that, as I lay in bed battling against insomnia, a new idea occurred to me. Not an idea, perhaps, but a thought, a little notion. I had been reading a lot of detective novels that year, mostly of the hard-boiled American school, and beyond finding them to be good medicine, a balm against stress and chronic anxiety, I had developed an admiration for some of the practitioners of the genre. The best ones were humble, no-nonsense writers who not only had more to say about American life than most so-called serious writers, but often seemed to write smarter, crisper sentences as well. One of the conventional plot gimmicks of these stories was the apparent suicide that turns out to have been a murder. Again and again, a character would ostensibly die by his or her own hand, and by the end of the story, after all the tangled strands of the intrigue had finally been unraveled, it would be discovered that the villain was in fact responsible for the character's death. I thought: why not reverse the trick and stand it on its head?

Why not have a story in which an apparent murder turns out to be a suicide? As far as I could tell, no one had ever done it.

It was no more than idle speculation, a two-in-the-morning brain wave, but I couldn't fall asleep, and with my heart beginning to race and flutter in my chest, I pursued the thought a little further, trying to calm myself by cooking up a story to go with my curveball premise. I had no stake in the results, was simply groping for a sedative to tranquilize my nerves, but one piece of the puzzle kept fitting beside another, and by the time I drifted off to sleep, I had worked out the bare-bones plot of a mystery novel.

The next morning, it occurred to me that it might not be such a bad idea to sit down and write the damn thing. It wasn't that I had anything better to do. I hadn't written a decent syllable in months, I couldn't find a job, and my bank account was down to almost nothing. If I could crank out a reasonably good detective novel, then surely there would be a few dollars in it. I wasn't dreaming of bags of gold anymore. Just an honest wage for an honest day's work, a chance to survive.

I started in early June, and by the end of August I had completed a manuscript of just over three hundred pages. The book was an exercise in pure imitation, a conscious attempt to write a book that sounded like other books, but just because I wrote it for money doesn't mean that I didn't enjoy myself. As an example of the genre, it seemed no worse than many others I had read, much better than some. It was good enough to be published, in any case, and that was all I was after. My sole ambition for the novel was to turn it into cash and pay off as many bills as I could.

Once again, I ran straight into problems. I was doing everything in my power to prostitute myself, offering up my wares for rock-bottom prices, and still no one would have me. In this case, the problem wasn't so much what I was trying to sell (as with the game), but my own astonishing ineptitude as a salesman. The only editors I knew were the ones who hired me to translate books, and they were ill qualified to pass judgment on popular fiction. They had no experience with it, had never read or published books like mine, and were scarcely even aware that such a thing as mystery novels existed, let alone the assorted subgenres within the field: private-eye novels, police procedurals, and so on. I sent off my manuscript to one of these editors, and when he finally got around to reading it, his response was surprisingly enthusiastic. "It's good," he said, "very good. Just get rid of the detective stuff, and you'll have yourself an excellent psychological thriller."

"But that's the whole point," I said. "It's a detective novel."

"Maybe so," he said, "but we don't publish detective novels. Rework it, though, and I guarantee that we'll be interested."

Altering the book might have interested him, but it didn't interest me. I had written it in a specific way for a specific purpose, and to begin dismantling it now would have been absurd. I realized that I needed an agent, someone to shop the novel around for me while I took care of more pressing matters. The rub was that I didn't have the first idea how to find one. Poets don't have agents, after all. Translators don't have agents. Book reviewers who make two or three hundred dollars per article don't have agents. I had lived my life in the remote provinces of the literary world, far removed from the commercial center where books and money have something to say to each other, and the only people I knew were young poets whose work appeared in little magazines, publishers of small, not-for-profit presses, and various other cranks, misfits, and exiles. There was no one to turn to for help, not one scrap of knowledge or information available to me. If there was, I was too dumb to know where to find it. Quite by chance, an old high school friend mentioned that his ex-wife happened to run a literary agency,

and when I told him about my manuscript, he urged
me to send it to her. I did, and after waiting nearly a
month for an answer, I was turned down. There wasn't
enough money in this kind of thing, she said, and it
wasn't worth her trouble. No one read private-eye novels anymore. They were passé, old hat, a losing proposition all around. Word for word, it was identical to
the speech the game broker had given me not ten days
before.

Eventually, the book was published, but that didn't
happen until four years later. In the meantime, all
sorts of catastrophes occurred, one upheaval followed
another, and the last thing on my mind was the fate
of my pseudonymous potboiler. My marriage broke up
in November 1978, and the typescript of the money
novel was shoved into a plastic bag, all but lost and
forgotten through several changes of address. My father died just two months after that—suddenly, unexpectedly, without ever having been sick a day in his
life—and for many weeks the bulk of my time was
spent taking care of estate business, settling his af-
fairs, tying up loose ends. His death hit me hard,
caused immense sorrow inside me, and whatever energy I had for writing I used to write about him. The
terrible irony was that he had left me something in

his will. It wasn't a great amount as far as inheritances go, but it was more money than I had ever had before, and it helped see me through the transition from one life into another. I moved back to New York and kept on writing. Eventually, I fell in love and married again. In the course of those four years, everything changed for me.

Sometime in the middle of that period, in late 1980 or early 1981, I received a call from a man I had met once before. He was the friend of a friend, and since the meeting had taken place a good eight or nine years earlier, I could scarcely remember who he was. He announced that he was planning to start a publishing company and wondered if I happened to have a manuscript he could look at. It wasn't going to be just another small press, he explained, but a real business, a *commercial operation*. Hmmm, I said, remembering the plastic bag at the bottom of my bedroom closet, if that's the case, then I just might have something for you. I told him about the detective novel, and when he said that he would be interested in reading it, I made a copy and sent it to him that week. Unexpectedly, he liked it. Even more unexpectedly, he said that he wanted to go ahead and publish it.

I was happy, of course—happy and amused, but also a trifle apprehensive. It seemed almost too good to be true. Publishing books wasn't supposed to be so easy, and I wondered if there wasn't a catch to it somewhere. He was running the company out of his Upper West Side apartment, I noticed, but the contract I received in the mail was a real contract, and after looking it over and deciding that the terms were acceptable, I couldn't think of a reason not to sign it. There was no advance, of course, no money up front, but royalties would begin with the first copy sold. I figured that was normal for a new publisher just getting off the ground, and since he had no investors or serious financial support, he couldn't very well cough up money he didn't have. Needless to say, his business didn't quite qualify as a *commercial operation*, but he was hoping it would become one, and who was I to throw a wet blanket on his hopes?

He managed to bring out one book nine months later (a paperback reprint), but production of my novel dragged on for close to two years. By the time it was printed, he had lost his distributor, had no money left, and to all intents and purposes was dead as a publisher. A few copies made it into a couple of New York bookstores, hand-delivered by the publisher himself, but the rest of the edition remained in cardboard boxes, gathering dust on the floor of a warehouse somewhere in Brooklyn. For all I know, the books are still there.

Having gone that far with the business, I felt I should make one last effort and see if I couldn't conclude it once and for all. Since the novel had been "published," a hardcover edition was no longer possible, but there were still the paperback houses to consider, and I didn't want to walk away from the book until they'd had a chance to turn it down. I started looking for an agent again, and this time I found the right one. She sent the novel to an editor at Avon Books, and three days later it was accepted. Just like that, in no time at all. They offered an advance of two thousand dollars, and I agreed to it. No haggling, no counteroffer, no tricky negotiations. I felt vindicated, and I didn't care about the details anymore. After splitting the advance with the original publisher (as per contract), I was left with a thousand dollars. Deduct the ten percent agent's commission, and I wound up making a grand total of nine hundred dollars.

So much for writing books to make money. So much for selling out.

(1996)